THE ILLUSTRATED HISTORY OF
MICKEY MANTLE

George Loh

THE ILLUSTRATED HISTORY OF
MICKEY MANTLE

Gene Schoor

CARROLL & GRAF PUBLISHERS, INC

NEW YORK

Copyright © 1996 by Gene Schoor.

First edition 1996.

Carroll & Graf Publishers, Inc.
260 Fifth Avenue
New York, NY 10001

ISBN 0-1867-0305-9

Library of Congress Cataloging-in-Publication Data is available.

Manufactured in the United States of America.

Designed by C. Linda Dingler

To my lovely wife for these many years, Fran Schoor, always at my side to critique these stories.

ACKNOWLEDGMENTS

No story of the incredible career of Mickey Mantle, with a scope as wide as that of the national pastime, is possible without the help and cooperation of hundreds of people. That includes the great personal help the author has received in the past from one of the greatest baseball stars who ever lived, Mickey Mantle himself.

The very first time that Mickey came to New York in 1951, the author interviewed him for television and radio. Later, when Joe DiMaggio show went on the air, Mantle was a frequent guest on that program, produced by the author. So belatedly we thank Mickey for the great life he led and his magnificent career on the major league scene for some eighteen years.

And to the many stars, coaches, managers and individual sportswriters who took the time to answer our questions and to supply pertinent material to the most stirring moments of the life of Mickey Mantle.

To the sportswriters: Jimmy Breslin, Dick Schaap, Jimmy Cannon, Dick Young, Joe Durso, Al Buck, Leonard Cohen, Lee Allen, Jerry Mitchell, Milt Gross.

To the many sports people in and around Commerce, Oklahoma: Vicki Crawford, Marshall Smith, Mayor Jack Young, Bob Weisler, Joe Pollack, and John Hall.

Thank you to the following, who provided many of the photographs contained in this book: The Official files of the New York Yankees, the Associated Press, United Press, The Tri-State Tribune in Picher, Oklahoma, the Baseball Hall of Fame, The New York Post, Sporting News, Sport Magazine. And special thanks to my photo agent, the unbelievable Wayne Laroque for his uncanny ability to seek out photos of Mickey Mantle.

CONTENTS

THE ILLUSTRATED HISTORY OF
MICKEY MANTLE

1

BORN TO PLAY BASEBALL

The year 1931 was mostly an eventful year for the United States. There was a terrible depression and millions of people were out of work, but it wasn't the desperate depression yet that it would become in the mid-'30s.

Herbert Hoover was president of the United States, and in an effort to put the unemployed to work, Hoover asked Congress for an appropriation of $150 million for the construction of public works.... The Bank of New York, hard hit by the depression, closed 60 local branches, and as the depression worsened, banks all over the nation were forced to shut their doors.... In New York City, Mayor Jimmy Walker was charged with malfeasance in office, and petitions to have him removed as mayor were sent to Governor Franklin Roosevelt.... An experimental passenger train developed by Thomas A. Edison began regular runs from Hoboken to Montclair, New Jersey.... In the sports world, Army defeated Navy in the annual football battle between the two service schools, by a 14–7 score.... Twenty Grand won the Kentucky Derby, and the St. Louis Cards defeated Connie Mack's Athletics 4–3 in the World Series....

The world itself was mostly at peace, although Italy's Benito Mussolini was stirring up a great deal of problems.... A world disarmament conference was being arranged for 1932. Aviators Wiley Post and Harold Getty flew around the world in record time.... The George

Washington Bridge was formally opened to traffic, and the great Thomas Edison died on October 18, at age eighty-four....

And on October 20, 1931, in an inkblot of a town, Spavinaw, Oklahoma, population three hundred, a newborn boy was christened Mickey Charles Mantle, the Mickey for the Athletics' catcher, Mickey Cochrane....

The land in that northeastern corner of Oklahoma was very hard land, and men worked under it to make a living. All around were the "chat" piles, pebbly refuse mounds that came from the lead and zinc that had been extracted from the ore. The chat piles rose like mountains against the sky.

One of the miners in that dry, desolate area of America was a man named Charles Mantle. As a teenager he had played a lot of baseball. Even as a miner he played ball, both for money (with semipro teams) and as a release from the relentless drudgery of his brutal work. He was a left-handed pitcher and his son, Elven, grew up to be a right-handed pitcher and played on the same teams as his dad.

But there was never that much baseball for the Mantles.

Their life, and the life of most of the people in the neighborhood, revolved around the mines. The Mantle clan was pure Oklahoma, born and bred in the region called the tristate district because that part of the northeastern corner of Oklahoma comes close to the northwestern corner of Arkansas, and the southwestern corner of Missouri.

Elven Mantle went down to the mines like his dad, but in the back of his mind he cherished an abiding dream—that someday one of his own flesh and blood would grow up to be a great professional baseball player and escape the grim life of a miner.

Mantle told the dream more than once to the woman he chose to marry, a tall, spirited, handsome lady named Lovell Richardson. And Lovell allowed how it would be wonderful if it could ever work out that way.

2

MUTT'S BOY

Mutt Mantle (Mutt was his nickname) not only played ball, he followed the big leaguers, too. He favored no particular team but took a liking to Mickey Cochrane. In 1929 Cochrane batted .331 for the Athletics and the following year he batted .357, while a teammate, Al Simmons, was hitting .381 and leading the American League, and by then everyone figured that Cochrane was the best catcher in baseball.

This was good enough for twenty-year old Mutt who, when informed that his wife was carrying their first child, told her, "If it's a boy, we're gonna name him Mickey, after Mickey Cochrane."

In those early months of the boy's first year, Elven and his father kept a close eye on the offspring. They talked to each other more than once about what kind of an athlete the baby would turn out to be. As if to help matters along, when Mickey was six months old, Mutt ordered his wife to make a baseball cap to fit the baby's head. And two and a half years later, Mutt had his wife tailor a complete uniform for the boy, using Mutt's own uniform pants. Mickey doesn't remember when he got his first glove, but he does remember that it was a Joe Gordon model.

When Mickey was four years old, the family took up from Spavinaw and moved seventy miles to Commerce, a town with a population of twenty-five hundred. Now there were twin boys in the family, Roy and Ray, and Mutt found a better job as the ground boss in the Blue Goose No. 1 lead and zinc mine of the Eagle-Picher Mining Company.

Much of Commerce is built over the mines, and that included

Mantle's home. Mickey once told a visitor, "You know, there's a mine right under the chair you're sitting on. Three hundred feet down the men are working in the ground."

The family moved into a clapboard house at 319 Quincy Street. There was a backyard, where Mickey's father and grandfather could begin the boy's apprenticeship as a baseball player. Mickey began Central Grade School when he was six, and that was when he began a parallel education in baseball.

When Mickey returned from school one day he met his father and grandfather out in the backyard. They had a small bat and several tennis balls, and Mickey looked at them wonderingly.

Mutt, holding the bat, came up to his son.

"You take this bat," Mutt said, "and just try to hit the balls we throw you. Now, we won't throw them hard, so don't worry about getting hurt."

Mickey took the bat and swung at the air. It was a smooth, natural, right-handed swing for Mickey. He was a right-hander all the way.

"Now, there's one thing I want to tell you," Mutt said. "When I throw the ball, you go ahead and swing the way you're doing now. But when Grandpa throws the ball, I want you to turn around and swing the other way. Understand?"

Mickey did not quite understand, but he did what he was told. He would not understand that Mutt Mantle was trying to give his son an advantage. Later, Tom Greenwade, the scout who signed Mickey, once said, "Mutt Mantle knew more baseball than the father of any boy I ever signed."

Mutt knew that it would be to Mickey's advantage to be a switch-hitter. Against a left-handed pitcher, a right-handed batter is better off than a left-handed batter because the curve ball breaks toward him and he can follow it better with his eyes. Against a right-handed pitcher, a left-handed batter has the edge for the same reason—plus the fact that he can speed down to first-base line faster than if he were standing right-handed at the plate. The best time to develop a batter as a switch-hitter, Mutt reasoned, was when a boy was very young.

He was right, of course, but in those early days—Mutt pitching left-handed, Grandfather Charley pitching right-handed, and Mickey duti-fully swinging from both sides of the plate—the young boy was not too happy about his father's theory.

At first, Mickey just didn't like it at all. He felt unnatural swinging from the left side of home plate, and he tried on occasion to swing righty. Once during a sandlot game, he came to bat right-handed against a right-handed pitcher. His father, who happened to be watching, became very angry. He made Mickey leave the game and sent him home.

He barked at the boy, "Don't you ever put on that baseball uniform again until you switch-hit like I taught you."

Mickey complained once or twice to his mother about this switch-hitting, but she was on her husband's side. "You do what your father says," ordered Mrs. Mantle. "Someday you'll be glad you listened to your father."

The days went slowly at first for the six-year-old. He would get back home from school at three-thirty, change into his old clothes, and practice every day until it got dark. On rare occasions when Mutt was satisfied that the boy was learning, he would give Mickey a day off to go hunting and fishing. The youngster loved those sports.

But mostly it was hard work, swinging a bat from both sides of the plate, with the two devoted instructors taking turns throwing to the boy. And soon Mickey began to get the hang of hitting left-handed, and he lost his awkwardness and started driving the ball left-handed as well as he always did right-handed.

It went on like that past the school season, to the end of spring. There were days when Mickey would stay out four or five hours just hitting the ball. Mutt and Charley then began throwing curves to Mickey, and Mickey began hitting the twisting gyrations of that tennis ball almost as well as he hit a fastball.

After a year and a half, the tennis ball was replaced by a regular baseball. But to make it more fun for Mickey, his dad devised a scheme. A ground ball, a pop fly, a strikeout were outs. A line drive past the pitcher was a single, off the house it was a double, off the roof a triple, and into the next lot a home run. Mickey hit plenty of home runs in those early days, and as his skill and swing improved, so did his determination to become a big-league ballplayer.

Soon baseball became the biggest thing in his life. When he wasn't practicing with his dad and grandfather, he was talking baseball or listening to the radio broadcasts of the Cardinals' games. By the time he was ten years old, Mickey's schoolmates were joking about his incredible dedication to the game. "When it comes four in the afternoon," one jest went, "Mickey has to stop playing baseball and start practicing the game."

In his eleventh year, Mickey became a ninety-pound catcher for the Douthat, Oklahoma, team in the Pee Wee League. He was also the league's best hitter, though his catching could have been improved on.

"When he squatted down behind the plate," his mother recalled, "wearing that protector that was too big for him, you couldn't see his feet and about all you could see of him except for his arms were those two little eyes sticking out of the protector like a scared turtle looking out of the shell."

Yet Mickey became one of the Pee Wee League's best players. He could hit the ball farther than anyone, and he also had more drive and spirit than the other boys. "When he got a single," a Commerce neighbor recalled, "he would come back to the bench muttering, 'it should have been a double.'"

Mickey Mantle at age fourteen. The Commerce (Oklahoma) High School did not have a team, so Mickey played with Miami, Oklahoma, a member of the Ban Johnson League in 1945.

The following year, Mickey graduated to the Gabby Street League, and Mutt Mantle permitted his son to be switched from catcher to shortstop. By this time, Mickey's dad had other things on his mind.

He had moved his family—which now consisted of Mickey, the twin boys, Barbara, and a younger son, Larry—to the outskirts of Commerce. Charley had become ill and Mutt, to get him away from the mines, had bought some chickens, hogs, cows, and a tractor, and tried farming on 180 acres along the Neosho River.

It was a daring gamble on Mutt's part, but for the kids it was a holiday. "It made it a lot easier to hunt and fish," Mickey recalled. "I rode a horse to school, which was about ten miles away. He was sure an understanding horse. He didn't like school either. He loved to run away with me on his back and start grazing around some fishing hole."

In 1945, the year his grandfather died, and Mickey was fourteen years of age, he entered Commerce High School. He played basketball and informal baseball. The school did not have a regular baseball team, but that summer Mick played in the Junior Cardinal League in the American Legion Baseball program.

In 1946, Mickey played football for Commerce High and soon developed into the finest running back on the squad. One afternoon in practice, Mick was driving into the line with the ball, and in a pileup he was kicked hard in the shin of his left leg. He continued to play, but after practice the pain became much worse.

At home that night he was unable to sleep. In the morning he took one look at his leg and became frightened. The ankle had turned blue and was twice its normal size. Mutt rushed Mickey to the hospital, and the ankle was bandaged. But the next day, the pain was so bad that Mickey's coach at Commerce, Allen Woolard, called Mutt. "I think you should have Mickey see a bone specialist in Picher, and I don't like the way it looks. Don't waste any time. Do it now."

Mutt rushed his son to Picher, where the doctors examined the ankle and took X rays. In a little while, the doctor called Mutt aside. "Your son has a bone disease. It's called osteomyelitis."

"What does that mean, exactly?" said Mutt.

"Osteomyelitis," said the doctor, "is a bone infection. It produces chronic inflammation of the bones. We can treat it and help it, but we cannot cure it."

"You mean he'll always have it?" Mutt was staggered by the doctor's explanation.

"With treatment," said the doctor, "the pain and swelling will disappear. But it could come back. It could come back even if your son bruises the leg slightly."

"My son is a ballplayer," Mutt said slowly. "What can I do?"

"I would go to Oklahoma City. They have the very latest medical facilities. They can help you the most. But do it soon."

So Mutt and Mickey drove to Oklahoma City. Mickey was in the hospital for two weeks. The ankle was lanced, and Mick was given penicillin injections every three hours. At first the ankle did not respond, and the doctors actually considered the possibility of amputating Mickey's left leg. But finally, after Mutt and Mickey almost gave up, the swelling and pain subsided. The disease had been arrested. But it would be a problem for the rest of Mickey's life.

Mickey returned to Commerce on crutches in September 1946. He was an unhappy youngster and felt that his whole world had turned upside down. What would he do if he could never play ball again? Mutt Mantle felt almost as bad, and to cheer up his son, he splurged on two tickets to the opening game of the 1946 World Series in St. Louis, some three hundred miles from Commerce.

Those were the first two major-league games Mickey had ever seen,

When Mickey was not playing baseball or football, he and his brothers and sisters were at some pond in Commerce, fishing. Here's Mickey (center) with twin brothers Ray and Roy, and sister Barbara (in background), with a sample of their catch for the day.

and he was thrilled to the core as he watched the play of the Red Sox and the Cardinals. He saw the Sox come from behind in the tenth inning to win the game by a 3–2 score, and it was a home run by Rudy York of the Sox that won the game. Then the next day he saw his favorite team, the Cardinals, come back to defeat the Red Sox, 3–0, and watched open-mouthed as pitcher Harry Brecheen spun a marvelous four-hit shutout.

Mick and his dad returned to Commerce, and both were in a better frame of mind as they listened to the rest of the Series games on the radio.

Mick went back to school. He was finally able to throw his crutches away and was able to play basketball for Commerce. And in the spring he was well enough to play baseball once more.

He played football and became the finest halfback in the area, scoring 10 touchdowns in the seven games Commerce played.

In his senior year, Mickey blossomed as a batter. In a game against Miami Junior College, Mickey hit home runs from both sides of the plate as Commerce, won with ease, and by 1948 he began to play for the Baxter Springs Whiz Kids. He began to drive home runs to every corner of every park, and soon the scouts began to visit the Whiz Kids to watch Mickey in action.

3

TOM GREENWADE'S DISCOVERY

One day in August 1948, a Yankee scout, Tom Greenwade, stopped by to visit his friend Kay Jacobson.

"Tom, you've got to take a look at this kid Mantle. He's playing with Baxter Springs. He's a natural."

"How good?" asked Greenwade.

"He plays shortstop," said Jacobson, "and makes lots of errors. But he's got a great arm, fast as a streak, and he's a heck of a switch-hitter. Hits with real power either way."

"Where can I see him?"

"Come on over to Alba tomorrow. The Whiz Kids are playing there."

So Tom Greenwade, Yankee scout, got his first look at Mickey Mantle. Mickey played shortstop but did not impress Tom.

After the game Jacobson asked Greenwade, "What about Mantle?"

"I liked that kid on third base, Johnson. Mantle, not much to see there. But keep me posted."

In the spring of 1949, Jacobson caught up with Mantle—a Mantle he hardly recognized. Mickey had grown nearly three inches and put on twenty pounds and had that great seventeen-inch bull neck, and the smoothest batting swing he'd seen in a long time.

"What about baseball, Mick?" Jacobson asked.

Mickey grinned. "I play it all the time."

"Mick, I want you to go to Joplin and see Johnny Sturm. He manages the Yankee farm club there. Ask him to look you over. I'll tell him you're coming to see him."

A few days later, Mickey hitched a ride to Joplin, some thirty-three miles from Commerce, and went to see Sturm, who had been a Yankee first baseman in 1941.

At fifteen years of age, with the baby fat fading away, Mickey was now a star for the Miami team. His uncle Luther Richardson, a fine player and one of Mickey's early boosters, is shown with Mantle.

Mickey approached Sturm and said shyly, "Mr. Jacobson sent me."

"I know," said Sturm. "He told me all about you. Get on over to the clubhouse; we've got a uniform for you."

For two nights Mickey worked out at shortstop. He also hit against Joplin's Class C pitchers in batting practice. After the sessions were over, Sturm questioned Mickey.

"Mick, when do you finish high school?"

"In about two weeks."

"You looked pretty good out there. Nice, smooth swing. Go on home. You'll hear from us."

Mickey was speechless. He wanted to hang around to ask Sturm a hundred questions. Would the Yankees sign him? Could he play shortstop? Could he play well enough for Class C? But he was scared and thrilled. He went home still wondering, and worrying about his chances.

Three weeks went by and Mickey's heart was sick.

Nobody called.

Then unexpectedly, Tom Greenwade called Mutt Mantle.

"Mutt," said Greenwade, "I'd like to take another look—what's the Baxter schedule look like?"

"The Whiz Kids are playing Coffeyville again on Sunday at Baxter Springs. Maybe you ought to watch them."

"I'll be there," said Tom.

It was a warm, humid, cloudy night in Baxter Springs when the Whiz Kids took the field against Coffeyville. The air hung heavily over the diamond. Greenwade sat next to Mutt Mantle as the game began. Mickey came to bat in the first inning and batted right-handed against pitcher Carl Pevelhuge, a southpaw.

It was the first time Greenwade had seen Mickey bat right-handed.

"He do that all the time?" Greenwade asked, forgetting that he had been told that Mantle was a switch-hitter.

"All the time," said Mutt. "Since he was as high as the seat we're sitting on."

The first pitch came into Mickey, and he drove it on a line for a double. Greenwade just mumbled to himself.

He played a good game, got a couple more hits, and just as the game ended, it started to rain. Mutt and Mickey took shelter in Tom's car.

Greenwade looked at Mickey and smiled. "At least you look like a ballplayer." Mickey grinned and dropped his head.

"I think you'll be okay," Greenwade said, patting Mantle on the shoulder. Then Mutt began to speak, but Greenwade stopped him short.

"I can pay Mickey $140 a month on a Class D contract," he said.

Mutt shook his head. "Tom, he can make more than that in the

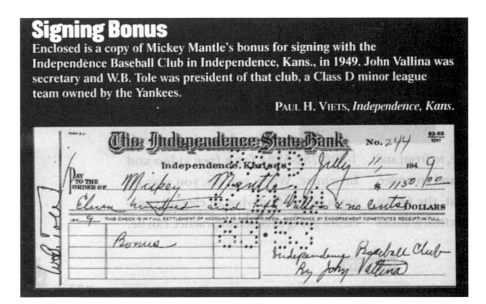

Signing Bonus

Enclosed is a copy of Mickey Mantle's bonus for signing with the Independence Baseball Club in Independence, Kans., in 1949. John Vallina was secretary and W.B. Tole was president of that club, a Class D minor league team owned by the Yankees.

PAUL H. VIETS, *Independence, Kans.*

Left: A copy of the check Mickey Mantle received for signing with the Yankees in 1949.

Below: Early in 1949, Yankee scout Tom Greenwade (center) was tipped off about the abilities of a young phenomenon playing ball in the Oklahoma-Missouri League with a team in Baxter Springs. After watching Mickey hit safely from both sides of the plate, driving the ball with great power, Greenwade offered Mickey a bonus of $1,100, plus $140 a month. In the photo, Greenwade is shown with pitcher Ralph Terry and Mantle in 1949.

mines. He can make 87½ cents an hour and play once a week at Spavinaw for $15 a game. And all the teams around here want him to play."

"Well, let's see, then," Tom said. He took out a Yankee contract and began making a few notes. "Now, here's the best I can do. I can give him a bonus of $1,100 and $140 a month as salary for the rest of the season. That comes to $1,450. Any more money and he has to be classified as a bonus baby. I'll put him with Independence after a week or so at Bransom to keep an eye on him. He'll get plenty of coaching there."

"And then what about next year?" Mutt asked.

"If he can handle Class D ball, we'll boost him and send him to Joplin. That's close to home and we'll give him plenty of schooling. If he's got it there, we'll move again."

"Well, Mick, how do you feel about this?" Mutt asked.

Mickey looked at his dad; his eyes were misty. "If you feel it's all right, then that's it. It's sure okay with me."

And so it was done on a day that Mickey remembered for the rest of his life.

On a dank, rainy night in a parked Buick sedan in a tiny town of midwestern America, the dream was fulfilled for the father—and the son.

And the Yankees?

They made for themselves one of the most fabulous deals in their history. For in an era when bonus babies were being signed for $75,000 and $100,000, the Yankees picked off the prize of prizes for a pittance.

They had selected a youngster who one day would be placed alongside Babe Ruth, Lou Gehrig, and Joe DiMaggio, and who would become the most explosive, dynamic, and one of the most popular ballplayers in Yankee history.

4

DiMAGGIO AND
THE REPORTERS

The army of reporters gathered around Joe DiMaggio at the preseason training camp of the Yankees in the spring of 1951, like
bees around a cluster of honey. DiMag was not only the biggest
man in that early camp session, he also was the biggest man in the game,
and what he had to say was big news. And what Joe had to say was just
what the Yankee fans wanted to hear back home, to read, digest, and to
discuss and argue about with other fans.

"Another big year for you, Joe?" asked Milt Gross of the *New York
Post*.

Joe's poker face broke into a wide grin. "If I have another one like
last year, I'll die a very happy man."

"Yeah, for sure," said Al Buck, another writer. "Those thirty-two
home runs and all those extra-base hits won a lot of games near the end
of the season, despite those bad feet of yours."

Surgery on his aching heel had prevented Joe from playing ball for
the first three months of the 1949 season, and when he finally returned to
the lineup against the Red Sox at Fenway Park, Joe was hardly in playing
shape for this vital series.

Before 36,000 wild-eyed fans, and with his foot encased in a cush-
ion-spiked shoe, DiMag's three-run homer in the third inning provided
the winning runs. The next afternoon, with the Yankees trailing, 7–1, in

At the first prespring training camp that
manager Stengel inaugurated in 1951,
a horde of reporters surrounded Joe
DiMaggio and belabored him with the
question, "Is this the last year for you,
Joe?" DiMaggio was noncommital.

the fifth inning, Joe drove out a three-run blast, and his home run in the eighth inning won the game. The next day Joe delivered a mammoth three-run homer that delivered the *coup de grâce* for another Yankee win.

For all intents and purposes, the stunning sweep of this vital series dealt a body blow to the Red Sox and their pennant aspirations by one man: Joe DiMaggio.

DiMaggio's incredible one-man show made front-page news throughout the nation and so inspired his teammates that they raced to their first pennant and World Series title under Casey Stengel.

Again the following year, 1950, DiMaggio's 32 home runs and a barrage of extra-base hits sparked the Yankees to another pennant and World Series title.

"Yankee fans aren't worrying about you dying if you have another good year," said Bob Cooke of the *New York Herald Tribune*, "but they do want to know about you and your thoughts about the team and the new players, and about things in general."

"I think it'll be all right," said Joe thoughtfully. "But I'm not kidding myself. I can't keep playing this game forever. I'm not a kid anymore, and every day it gets tougher and tougher, and every part of my body aches. But I think I've got another good season left, maybe two. I've had a long run in the game, longer than most players."

Then, right in the middle of the discussion, there was a tremendous CRACK! as a bat crashed into a pitched ball.

All heads turned to watch the flight of the ball.

"Holy cats!" one of the writers shouted. "That drive went about four hundred feet!"

"A home run in any ballpark," said DiMaggio.

Then they all turned in the direction of home plate.

"Don't tell me that rookie belted that ball," said the reporter.

"It sure looks like it," said DiMaggio.

"Casey has a heck of a lot of good-looking kids to work with this year. And three or four of them look like they may make it back to New York and stay with us, including the kid who hit that ball. His name's Mantle, Mickey Mantle," said Joe. "Hits the ball with tremendous power, and he's a real nice kid."

"Probably a lucky wallop," one hard-boiled reporter said. "The kid will probably go through life wondering how he ever knocked that one out of the park."

Mickey Mantle seemed to explode out of a bottle as he drove another shot over the fence. Again and again he drove into each pitch that resounded all over the practice session. Now all the players just stood open-mouthed as the big, broad-shouldered rookie rattled the fence as he sprayed ball after ball to all fields.

As the regular players trooped into the training camp at Phoenix, Arizona, they heard stories of the fence-busting rookie. Now they wanted to see him in action. They wanted to know more about this husky, blond, baby-faced slugger from Oklahoma. Mickey himself didn't quite know what to say to such great stars as Phil Rizzuto, Yogi Berra, Bill Dickey, and DiMaggio, and they tried to put him at ease.

But it was Yogi Berra, the Yankee catcher, who cornered Mickey in the Yankee clubhouse.

"Where you from, kid?" Yogi asked.

"Commerce, Oklahoma," Mickey said.

"That a big city?"

"No, Mr. Berra. Population about twenty-three hundred," said Mantle. "But it's only about seven miles to Joplin. That has about ten thousand people. That's a bigger city. Has a good ball-club, too."

At the 1951 prespring training camp, DiMaggio posed with the newest Yankee sensation, young Mickey Mantle. "Is this where you get all that power, Mickey?" Joe asked. Mantle, too shy to answer, just shook his head and grinned.

Phil Rizzuto also talked with Mantle. "What position, Mickey?"

"Shortstop," said Mantle. "But you have nothing to worry about. I make too many errors, like I did when I played in the Western League."

"Hey, Casey," a reporter called to the Yankee manager, "give us the rundown on this new kid, Mantle. Everyone is calling him the 'new DiMaggio.'"

Manager Casey Stengel did a little dance as he came over to a group of reporters. "Friends, we've got dancin' weather today. Every time we get a player that hits 'em a mile, why, it's dancin' weather," said Casey with a smile.

"Now, this kid is peacock green. He's just nineteen years old and still growing. He was down playing with Joplin last year," said Casey, "and he broke the league up with his hitting. I think he hit about .320, and half his hits were extra-base shots. He comes from poor mining people and he ain't any more anxious to work in a regular job than you guys. So he played shortstop. Pretty bad, too. Year before that, he idled a season away with a team in the Independence League. That's Class D ball. And just before that, he was playing in high school and learnin' his readin' and writin'. Now, you can see he's just a little schoolboy, still learnin'."

"That's all the experience this kid's got? Case, how could you bring a green kid like Mantle up here?" said a reporter. "That's never been done before."

"Well," said Casey, "how in hell and how much experience did you have when you were nineteen?"

"Now, maybe he's got it in him to be a big leaguer, and then again, maybe he ain't," said Casey. "But I'm way ahead of you fellas. I know what you're saying." Then he started to imitate the hard-nosed reporter's voice:

"Old Casey got the luck. Come to the Yankees in '49. DiMaggio starts limpin'. So Tommy Henrich starts battin' like DiMag and makes Casey look real good. Then DiMag makes a great comeback and Casey's got a pennant and World Series. This year, The Old Perfessor's dead. Dead as a dodo. That's what you say. And to make sure, you'd like to load me up with a bunch of raw rookies and me finishing in last place."

"Casey," said the reporter, "you're way off beam."

"Man off his beam don't win two World Series in a row," said Stengel. his eyes glistening. Then he danced away.

And then on March 2, in a historic press interview with several reporters, Joe DiMaggio told of his plans for retiring.

"I want to have one good year and then hang 'em up for good," DiMaggio said. "And it will have to be this year."

The next day, Mickey Mantle was moved from his shortstop post to the outfield, with Tommy Henrich assigned to teach Mickey the vagaries of outfield play.

"His hands are not right for shortstop," said Casey. "He's too tense and he's got the most erratic arm I've ever seen. Most of the time he throws the ball into the seats trying to make a play at first."

Tommy Henrich worked hard with Mantle. Mickey knew nothing about playing the outfield. He didn't know how to use his sunglasses. He

Mickey Mantle reported to the Yankees in 1951 as a shortstop, but after watching Mickey play at that position, Stengel decided that he would shift Mantle to the outfield. Stengel assigned Yankee star Tommy Henrich the job of teaching the vagaries of outfield play to Mickey. In the photo, Mickey listens as Henrich suggests and watches Mickey grasp a bat.

didn't know how to throw from the outfield, and he would allow fly balls to drop and chase them as they rolled and rolled and rolled.

It was not easy for Mickey. He had never played there, but under Henrich's steadying hand, he gradually improved.

"One thing about outfield play is that you get lots of chances to run. You have to run like hell to get some of those drives, and I get a lot of satisfaction out of that," Mickey said. "I like to run, could run all day."

Inside of a week, and after Henrich had worked every angle of outfield play with Mickey and had hit hundreds of fungoes to the right and the left of Mantle, Henrich said Mickey was ready to play in exhibition games.

In one of the first games, against the White Sox, a batter hit a long fly ball to Mantle. Mickey raced back, back and caught the ball on his right hip and, in the same motion, ripped the ball to the plate. The perfect throw prevented Jim Busby, who was on third base, from scoring. At the end of the inning, Henrich came out to greet Mickey.

"Mickey, just forget most of what I've tried to teach you about getting throws off in a hurry. That last play was a thing of beauty. Just continue to do it the way you just did."

Early in March, Stengel, in a talk to reporters said, "As far as his hitting is concerned, he's a big leaguer right now. The kid is absolutely tremendous. The pitchers don't know how to pitch to him. One time he hits the fence right-handed, then the next time he comes up lefty and hits the ball over the wall. He's the best switch-hitter I've ever seen."

"We'll see how Mantle does against the pros when the real exhibition games begin."

The Yankees went on a swing through California, and West Coast fans got a close-up of the phenom they had been reading about. And they were not disappointed.

Casey kept thinking of John McGraw and Mel Ott. McGraw was in his fifties when one of his baseball friends sent Ott to the New York Giants when Mel was just sixteen. Ott was a prize, and McGraw nurtured him. Every baseball fan learned that McGraw refused to send Ott to the minors for fear that some inept manager would ruin the boy's magnificent but unorthodox swing. (Ott lifted his forward foot off the ground as he prepared to swing.) Ott sat on the bench next to manager McGraw for a year or two before becoming the National League's home-run king. Mel played for a dozen years after McGraw's death, and no one ever forgot that he was McGraw's boy.

Now Stengel wanted somebody like that. He could boast about teaching a Martin or a Lopez, but Casey had never produced a great player who was his boy as Ott was McGraw's. Now he had him—a youngster with Cobb's speed and Ruth's power, raw material with the potential to be the greatest player of all time, just waiting to be taught by Stengel.

Casey Stengel envied the great record and career of the immortal John McGraw of the New York Giants. Casey had played for McGraw in 1921-23 and was envious about McGraw's ability to develop young stars. McGraw had taken sixteen-year-old Mel Ott and developed him into one of the greatest players in the game. Now Stengel had his own eighteen-year-old in Mickey Mantle and wanted to make Mantle just as great as, if not greater than, Ott.

Casey, speaking to a friend, said, "Can you imagine what McGraw would say if he saw this kid?"

The question nearly became academic because just at that time, Mantle received a notice to report to his draft board in Miami, Oklahoma. They wanted Mickey back for another (his second) physical examination. Mickey had been examined six months earlier and had been classified 4-F because of his osteomyelitis, but now that he had become a celebrity, his local draft board was inundated with letters and calls about his failure to serve in the Armed Forces.

Mickey reported to his draft board on April 11, was examined thoroughly, and again was classified unfit for military service. He was classified 4-F. He then rejoined the team.

At Gilmore Stadium, in Hollywood, Mickey had the crowd roaring as he drove out several of the longest drives ever seen. Batting left-handed, the Mick hit eight drives into the boulevard behind the right-field fence in batting practice.

The following day, in a game at Wrigley Field, in Los Angeles, Mickey hit two drives that measured more than 400 feet each, and as the exhibition tour continued, Mickey's long drives in every ballpark continued to be the main topic of conversation, and overnight the glare of publicity moved from Joe DiMaggio's activities to the nineteen-year-old named Mickey Charles Mantle. And the sportswriters simply went wild over this corn-fed kid from Oklahoma.

Now, as the spring training games were nearing an end, the question on everybody's lips was whether this green kid would start the season in New York with the Yankees. Could it be possible that he would make the miraculous jump from someplace in Joplin to the World Champion Yankees?

Mickey and his dad, Mutt Mantle, discuss Mickey's progress with the Yankees in 1951, as they stand on the porch of the Mantles' tiny four-room cottage in Miami, Oklahoma.

Mantle in 1949, brothers Ray and Roy, Barbara, mother, father, and Larry.

Mantle, whom many believed was the greatest home-run prospect in a long time, is shown here in fielding form. Casey Stengel, manager of the Yankees, said that Mantle was a likely successor to the great Joe DiMaggio. DiMaggio hinted that he might hang up his spikes at the end of the 1951 season.

Could Mickey Mantle become the Frank Merriwell of the 1950s?

Casey Stengel said yes. He was even heard to say on more than one occasion, after seeing Mickey outrace the three fastest Yankees and run the bases in thirteen seconds, "My God! The boy runs faster than *Ty Cobb*!"

George Weiss, the Yankees' general manager, was well aware of Mantle's potential and was planning to send Mickey back to the minor leagues for further seasoning. But Stengel wanted to keep Mickey on the big club.

Mickey returned to New York after another visit to his draft board in time for the three final exhibition games, against the Dodgers in Brooklyn.

In the first game against the Dodgers, Mickey, still in a daze about playing against the great National League stars, could get only a single in four at-bats. In the second game, feeling better, he singled against pitcher Joe Hatten. Later, batting right-handed off Joe Romano, Mickey got two more singles. In the eighth inning, batting left-handed, Mickey drove a pitch over the scoreboard for a home run. He had four hits in five at-bats in this game. He finished the exhibition season with 41 hits in 102 at-bats, including seven doubles, one triple, and nine home runs, for a .402 batting average.

That night, the final question was solved as Mickey sat in a drawing room of a speeding express train on its way to Washington, D.C., for a series against the Senators. Mickey sat next to Yankee owners Dan Topping and Del Webb, and Yankee general manager George Weiss, and signed a Yankee contract for slightly more than the usual $6,000. Mickey received $7,500. It was more money than he had ever seen in his life. As a matter of fact, the contract had to be cosigned by Mickey's dad, Mutt Mantle, for Mickey was underage to sign a formal contract.

From Union Station in Washington, Mickey, along with baseball writer Tom Meany, rode in a taxi to the Shoreham Hotel. As the cab passed the illuminated dome of the White House, Mickey gazed at it in awe.

"So this is our nation's capital," he said to Meany.

He was still very much the wide-eyed, fresh, American country kid, only now he was on the edge of the biggest adventure in his life. That night in his hotel room, awaiting the 1951 opening game against the Senators, Mickey lay in his bed unable to believe that come the next day he would wear the uniform of the World Champion New York Yankees. And sleep was the farthest thing in his mind.

Here he was in a magnificent hotel room, with all expenses paid, money . . . more money in his pockets than he had ever had in his life, money to pay off the mortgage on the Mantle home in Commerce . . . enough money to never have to go down some three hundred feet to work in the mines back home. He was unable to sleep.

What would happen in that first game? And in the games and the years to come? How would he do? Would he fall on his face, or rise to the occasion?

Because he didn't know, and couldn't know, he felt he was lost in a great forest.

But he comforted himself by thinking: You're playing alongside the great Joe DiMaggio, Phil Rizzuto, Johnny Mize, Allie Reynolds, Ed Lopat, Vic Raschi. You're playing with these guys . . . guys you only dreamed about. And now you're one of them.

You can't be too bad.

Mickey was having doubts about playing with the Yankees alongside DiMaggio, Rizzuto, Mize, and Reynolds.

5

EXPRESSWAY
TO THE YANKEES

Ten days after signing the contract with Tom Greenwade, Mickey bade his family good-bye and was on his way to Bransom, Missouri, a Yankee tryout camp where he could have a few days of indoctrination. Then he would be on his way to Independence, Missouri, for the Yankees' Class D team in the Kansas-Oklahoma-Missouri League.

Mantle arrived at Bramson on June 6, 1949, and was immediately taken in hand by a couple of tough veteran former major-league stars: Burleigh Grimes, a once-great spitball pitcher, and Dutch Zwilling.

"After six days with Grimes and Zwilling," said Mickey, "I was just about ready for my next stop, Independence. But when I got to Independence, I was actually more advanced than most of the players there. I met Harry Craft, who had many years as a major leaguer at Cincinnati and other teams in the late thirties and forties. Craft had a batting average of .253, but the figure didn't indicate the story of the man's complete mastery of the game. It was his complete knowledge and ability to work with young players that convinced the Yankees that [that] was the place for me."

Now Mickey Mantle, seventy-five miles away from home, was completely on his own as a ballplayer, and it was a new world that this seventeen-year-old had to adjust to.

"I didn't tell Dad that I was afraid to leave home. I guess there was no substitute for Mom's coffee and grits and bacon that only she could make for us kids. And now the thought of me being away from home for more than a day scared me hollow.

"Actually, the KOM League covered the neighborhood. Miami, Oklahoma, then in the league, was no farther away than the fancy stores. Carthage, Missouri, was thirty-five miles away from Commerce, and Pittsburgh, Kansas, about forty. Independence, Kansas, my new team, was just seventy-five miles away from the Blue Goose No. 1 mine, where Dad was a ground boss.

"Still, I felt like a foreigner. Dad kidded me about losing my citizenship. He also promised that he and the family would show up at the games every night no matter in what town we played.

"I played shortstop for about a week before Harry Craft called me aside for my first bit of professional instruction. I'd hit a couple of home runs and felt kind of swellheaded for a 17½-year-old kid.

"'Mickey,' he said, 'you'll never advance much higher in baseball if you don't learn to keep your head up when you return to the dugout at the close of an inning. You act as if you're ashamed of yourself. Yankees don't conduct themselves like that. Act like a champion and someday you might even play like one.'

"Craft spotted my most glaring weakness right from the beginning. I wasn't afraid of the crowds as long as I didn't have to look at the customers, especially after I failed in the clutch or pulled a skull in the field. And I really came up with my share. So to get around it, I would double up like a worm on a fishing hook and sneak into the dugout.

"'Straighten up,' Craft would say. 'Nobody is going to arrest you because you made an error. Take a look at the big-league box scores tonight and you'll note that some clubs committed more errors than we did.'

"Sometimes I thought I couldn't straighten up with a broomstick in my back. Even later on, when I made the big club in New York, and when I trotted back to the bench, my head was twisted to the left and jerked down as if I had a crick in my neck.

"I never could face folks if I was a side attraction, much less the center of it. I knew it from the time they talked me into appearing in a senior high school play. And would you listen to the name of the play: *Starring the Stars*. They even sold tickets to it. And I was very good, too.

"Harry Craft taught me the real meaning of hustle. I know it's old hat and you hear about the 'ole hustle' until you're sick of it. But not the way I learned it from Harry. Here is an example: How many times have you seen a batter barely trot down to first base after popping up? I know it's almost a sure thing to be caught. So you think, 'Why waste the energy?'

"That didn't go in Craft's book. Harry managed under the theory of taking advantage of that 'sure shot' when and if it came in. He declared that it's just the breaks that win pennants. So Harry ordered players to run them out all the way.

"Personally, after those orders from Harry, I always try to run hard as I can for two bases, and sometimes I would be the winning run on second base. That's one of the reasons I hit .322 in 87 games at Independence. I got 101 hits in 314 trips, 15 doubles, seven triples, and seven homers, and I batted in 63 runs.

"At the time I hoped I wasn't kidding myself in believing these figures had a lot to do [with] winning me a trip to the Yankees' first school for farm prospects, at Phoenix, Arizona, in February 1950.

"I hoped at the time I was not kidding myself in believing all of this, but I did try to do everything Harry Craft told me to."

Craft drove Mickey hard all season long because he fully realized the youngster's marvelous potential, and at the end of the season, after Independence ran away with the KOM Championship, Craft sent an enthusiastic letter to the Yankees' front office.

"Mickey Mantle can be a truly great hitter," the report began. "He's got exceptional bat speed, has great arm and wrist length, and is one of the fastest ballplayers I've ever seen. Even when he miffs a ball, like a jackrabbit he pounces on the ball and fires it to a base. But he's just an average shortstop, and *lets the ball play him* too much. Has an excellent attitude and I'm certain will go all the way to the big leagues. He has everything to make a truly great player. But I would like to see him shifted to third or perhaps the outfield."

Years later, Harry Craft looked back on those days and made a further assessment of young Mantle.

"He could hit the hell out of the ball, but had plenty to learn even though he learned quickly. It was obvious that he would never be a good shortstop. He made too many errors, and his arm was awful. But his real weakness was his temperament. He acted as if the whole world was coming to an end just because he made a few errors or struck out in the clutch."

6

DREAMS OF
A YANKEE ROOKIE

Mickey celebrated his eighteenth birthday that October of 1949 with his ma and pa back in Commerce. He took a job as an electrician's helper in Blue Goose No. 1, the same mine as his dad.

All that fall and winter, working some three hundred feet deep in the bowels of the earth, Mickey's mind was far away from Commerce, Oklahoma, and the mines. He dreamed of baseball, and his future with the Yankees. And he also wondered, with some anxiety, whether he would be good enough to make it—whether he would ever be good enough to be a Yankee.

But those long winter days were made far shorter by a few things. In his time off, Mickey went out and did a lot of hunting. He was especially fond of hunting rabbits in the snow. Later, when he became a Yankee, he would tell his teammates how he used to chase rabbits back in Commerce.

"I'd be fair to them," Mick would say with a straight face. "I'd chase them in the snow and wouldn't wear spikes or sneakers, and I'd give them a fair start."

One Sunday afternoon, when Mickey and a friend had an off day, they went to a high school football game between Picher and Farland. Each had a date. The friend's date was Merlyn Johnson, a pretty Picher drum majorette. Merlyn at that time had a bigger reputation than

Mickey. She sang solo at the First Baptist Church in Picher, and she also sang at nearby Army camps.

A few days later, Mickey went over to Picher. He had a date with a girlfriend of Merlyn's. The three dating couples drove out into the country. The two other boys kidded around, but Mickey was very quiet this day. Once in a while, though, Merlyn caught his eye, and he grinned at her.

That night after the date, Mickey came home and exclaimed not about his date, but about Merlyn. He told his mother, "I met the cutest little girl in Picher. She twirls the baton for the Picher band and she's got cute freckles."

The next day Merlyn got a phone call from her sister Pat's boyfriend. "Mickey Mantle wants a date with you," the boy said. Merlyn was annoyed that Mickey hadn't called himself, but agreed to a date. After three dates, Merlyn became Mickey's steady girlfriend. A few months later, Mickey bought Merlyn a ring.

Mickey's anxiety about his baseball future brightened considerably early in January 1950, when he received a letter from New York. It was from Lee MacPhail, director of the Yankees' farm system.

Mickey tore open the letter eagerly. Would Mickey Mantle like to attend a special school in February at Phoenix, Arizona, a school for the Yankees' best minor-league prospects?

"Frankly, I thought that was pretty good going for a fellow who had only half a season of Class D ball under his belt," said Mickey. "Other young players who reported to Phoenix included

Above: It is December 20, 1951, and after a marvelous first year with the New York Yankees, twenty-year-old Mickey Mantle, who has the job of filling the retired Joe DiMaggio's shoes as the Yankee center fielder, happily poses with Merlyn Johnson, his high school sweetheart and future bride.

Right: At a special instructional school set up by Casey Stengel in Phoenix, Arizona, in 1951 for "new prospects," with Yankee stars Yogi Berra, Phil Rizzuto, Bill Dickey, and Frank Crosetti acting as instructors, the young Mickey Mantle stepped up to bat. Suddenly, all activity stopped. Batting left and right, Mantle had the Yankee stars and Stengel amazed with his power.

  THE ILLUSTRATED HISTORY OF MICKEY MANTLE

Yankee coach Frank Crosetti discusses Mantle's play in the field in 1951 at Phoenix, Arizona.

Jackie Jensen, then a pitching hopeful, Jim Brideweser, a shortstop like myself, and a couple of other kids. That first day was an eye-opener to me.

"There was plenty to see and do. Besides manager Stengel, there were coaches like Bill Dickey, Frankie Crosetti, Jim Turner, and established Yankee stars like Yogi Berra, Hank Bauer, and Cliff Mapes, all of whom were listed as instructors.

"But the camp was a great experience for me. It was two weeks of close-up contact and practice with real, honest-to-goodness major-league stars. And my first to listen to the most amazing guy in baseball, Casey Stengel.

"Casey greeted us rookies with a speech. It was my introduction to that strange language known as 'Stengelese.' All I learned from his first oration is that 'you fellers have got a chance if you learn something about baserunning.'

"During the first week of the usual fundamentals, all I got from Stengel was an occasional wink and half a smile. But it wasn't until I won a footrace held among the rookies that Casey honored me with his first personal conversation. I listened and listened and listened, and I could not make any sense at all out of his talks.

"But after he was through talking, he got Crosetti and Berra and Bill

Dickey working us until our tongues hung out. I practiced and picked up some great advice. That's one of the Yankee secrets.

"Then following the last intrasquad game, a game in which I hit some great balls over the fence, the Yankees told me to go back home and await transportation to Lake Wales, Florida, where I was to get further training with the Kansas City club.

"I felt so good I telephoned Commerce and told the folks all about it. I realized I was going to Florida for more help and instruction, but it made me feel—almost like a Yankee. A little one anyway, because Dad told me on the phone it was a solid promotion.

"The promotion carried me from Class D to Class C to Joplin of the Western Association, where I continued to get the best in Yankee instructions.

"At Joplin, I could feel myself growing. By the time the middle of the season arrived (in my eighteenth year), my weight jumped to 180 and I stood 5-11, and I was getting some real distance to my drives. At mid-season I was clubbing everything that came my way and was hitting .414.

"When the season ended, I led the league with 26 home runs, 14 right-handed and 12 left-handed. I hit 12 triples, 30 doubles, batted in 135 runs, and hit .383 in 137 games.

"Near the end of our season, manager Craft called me over, put his arm around me, and said in a fatherly voice: 'Mickey, the Yankees want you to join the team in St. Louis. You'll stay with them for the entire month and might even get a chance to play in a few games. Now, keep doing what you've been doing down here and you could be a Yankee fixture.'

"Before I left for St. Louis, Harry Craft gave me the best advice yet, before he loaded me up with all kinds of encouragement about going places in the game. Harry said, 'You're going to make a lot of new and influential friends as you advance in this game of baseball. But remember this: Don't forget your old ones. They're the ones who made you.'

"On my way to St. Louis, I was happier than a barefoot boy who had shot his first quail. But when I got there I would have run all the way back home if anyone had hollered 'Git!' in the lobby of the Chase Hotel.

I only managed to get up a sweat in St. Louis because I was too afraid or too bashful to enter a batting cage during practice. But I was right on my hunch about not being another Rizzuto at shortstop. Phil was great to me and showed me enough infield drills to give me the idea that maybe I ought to try and make it at some other position. Dad had already discussed this with Harry Craft about my trying the outfield.

"But all the rest of it—the excitement, traveling with the great Yankees, DiMaggio, Bauer, Berra, Dickey, and all the big cities. Frankly, I was in a complete daze.

"Somehow I got through it all. I don't know how, I just did.

"In Chicago I met Moose Skowron, a big, husky college kid from Purdue University, and we roomed together as nonroster players. We took batting practice and infield practice with the team and then sat on the bench during the games. And that was a thrill.

"Chicago was Moose's hometown, so he showed me the sights. We'd wander along Michigan Avenue and inevitably find ourselves in the Loop, staring at the bright lights of movie houses. I guess we saw every movie there, whether the picture was bad or good. It didn't matter. When you're just eighteen years old and suiting up with the greatest major-league players, with your best days still ahead, every movie was great.

"I kind of followed Moose's lead during our week's stay with the team, such as waiting until he said something to one of the regular Yankee players, before I'd even open up my mouth.

"With Joe DiMaggio within easy reach every day, I couldn't even mumble hello. He had this air about him—this thing about, well, almost like a god. So I'd just keep looking at him, like sideways, and keep looking, and I imagine he got tired of looking at my face always turned toward his. A couple of times he even nodded at me. The truth was, I'd be thinking, God, wouldn't it be wonderful if I could ever play like him?

"But everything has an end, and soon my honeymoon (steak three times a day if you wanted) and the richest kind of train luxury and hotel living soon ended just before the Yankees headed back to New York and another World Series.

"Casey Stengel pulled me aside and said he'd be seeing me at the Phoenix early season school again in February 1951. I told him I could stand more schooling and said my good-byes. And then I headed back to Commerce, riding on a cloud of dreams to pass the winter and wait for another dream trip with the Yankees."

Only this time it would be different. Mickey would report to Phoenix not as a student in a rookies' school, but as a rookie working out with the Yankee regulars. He would get a chance to met Joe DiMaggio, talk with him, and have a chance to show the rest of the Yankee greats what he could do.

"Came that February," said Mickey, "I could hardly contain myself. Every morning I raced to the post office to inquire about that Yankee

In 1950, after Mickey hit 26 home runs with the Joplin team and led the league, he was invited to travel with the Yankees during the last month of the season. When the team got to Chicago, Mickey met another Yankee rookie, an ex-football star from Purdue University. Moose Skowron made it easier to talk to Yankee stars, for he had been around them longer. So Mickey began to relax and enjoy this marvelous opportunity.

Mantle became friendly with Yankee Cliff Mapes. When Mickey told Mapes that he had worked in the mines back home at Commerce, Mapes traveled to Commerce to see for himself. In the photo, Mutt Mantle, a crew boss at the Blue Goose No. 1 Mine, took Mapes (center) and Mickey down some three hundred feet and showed Mapes the way the miners worked each day.

notice to report to Phoenix. But I waited and waited and waited—and no report came. The Yankees had forgotten all about me.

"Finally, one day while working at the Blue Goose No. 1, I got a long-distance phone call from Yankee scout Johnny Neun: 'Mickey, what in thunder is the matter? What are you doing in the mines? You're supposed to be here in Phoenix!'"

Mickey was silent for a moment. Then he stammered, "Mr. Neun, I don't have enough money to get there."

"Then why in hell didn't you call or write us and say so? Do you expect the Yankees to hold spring training until next winter? Now, I'll wire the money as soon as I hang up. Now, get your bags packed and hop on the train the minute the Western Union boy walks in with the money."

"My suitcase has been packed for a month, Mr. Neun."

7

BROOKLYN
IS WONDERFUL

Brooklyn is wonderful even if it hasn't got any fish hatcheries in Prospect Park, but I wouldn't advise any nineteen-year-old country boy to play his first big-league game in Ebbets Field. That is, if he can't help it, and in April 1951, after I flew all night from home to get to the place.

"Casey Stengel noticed I looked sort of peaked. He thought I was tired from my long airplane ride, and asked me if I wanted another day off to get my bearings straight. When I told him I felt okay, he looked at the stands and chuckled. 'Fans over here might seem a little different to you,' he said. 'But they won't bite you. Do you know, I played the outfield with the Giants over here way back in 1912 and they liked me so much they didn't fire me until 1927. Then they brought me back as manager in 1934 and fired me in 1936. But they were so crazy about me, they paid me for doing nothing in 1937 and '38.'

"Stengel's talking to me eased me somewhat. He also explained to me that all those sportswriters on the field didn't mean any harm. I never did quite get it when he told me that all they wanted was a story from me, any kind of story, since that's the way they made a living. He also cackled something about not paying any attention to what the fans shouted.

"To tell you the truth, that's what bothered me. For after I got my first big-league hit, some guy popped up and screamed, 'Who do you think you are . . . DiMaggio? Ya bum!'

"Somebody told me, I forget who it was, that the fans would be a whole lot nicer in the Bronx. I didn't doubt it, but not when they're playing the Dodgers. Because I swear I heard that same fellow holler at me from the right-field stands in Yankee Stadium, 'I still say you can't carry Musial's glove, ya bum!' I wanted to break his goddamn neck even though I had to agree with him.

"I'd be lying if I denied reading the New York papers—all of them. And I must admit I noticed sports pages had me starting the 1951 season for the Yankees in right field. What puzzled me was that I didn't know—one way or the other. That's what made it so embarrassing. Sportswriters were asking me how I felt before I ever played it.

Casey Stengel meets with his top pitchers before the opening game of the 1951 season. L-R: Vic Raschi, Ed Lopat, Allie Reynolds, and Stengel.

"I never knew for sure until the night before we were scheduled to open in Washington. The team just pulled out of Penn Station when Casey called me into his private compartment on the train. It was after that meeting I learned that he had separate sets of languages—one for the press and one for his players.

"'I'm going to see how you look in right field tomorrow,' Stengel started. He was all business. 'Now, don't try to be what the writers say you are, because you can't be that good. Just don't be afraid, and you just hustle out there. That's one thing I'm sure about, your hustle. Now go back to your seat and don't even think about tomorrow. Just relax and have sweet dreams.'

"I thanked him and left and sat down and shook. I never stopped shaking all night, even in the swanky Shoreham Hotel. I wished that I could talk with Harry Craft, who managed me in Independence and at Joplin. He had been sent to manage Beaumont, which, to me, seemed to fit where I should be, instead of with the Yankees. As I said earlier, that's the way Dad and I had planned my career. And this seemed way over my head.

"The Washington game was postponed because of heavy rains, and the team returned to New York. I was glad and then got scared all over again when I suddenly realized we were going to play the first of two games with the Red Sox, the Yankees' great rivals. The game would be in the Stadium the very next day.

"No help. It didn't rain. And, sure enough, there was my name—

MANTLE—as big as you please, on the lineup card posted in the Yankee dugout. I was going to hit third behind Rizzuto, with Jackie Jensen leading off. DiMaggio hit clean-up and was followed by Yogi Berra, Johnny Mize, Billy Johnson, and Jerry Coleman, and Vic Raschi was the pitcher.

"As long as I live, I'll always remember that first-game lineup and the game, because it was my very first big-league game. I never thought I could make it to right field, for I was trembling. But Berra said something and got my blood moving again. He wasn't talking to anyone in particular. But I knew it would take more than a ball game, World Series, or rounders to upset Berra.

"'What kind of opening game is this?' beefed Yogi. 'Ain't no people here. The place is empty.'

"To me that sounded like a remark that a crazy man would make because I saw a lot of people—more people than I had ever seen in one place. Of course, the Stadium is a pretty big spot. There were about 45,000 fans there, and that's about twenty-five times the population of Commerce— a crowd big enough to make a rookie playing his first game a little bit on the tense side.

"Bill Wight started for the Red Sox, and the funny thing about it was that I wasn't worried so much about Wight, a good left-handed pitcher with a gosh-awful move to first base, as I was about Boston's left fielder.

"Ted Williams made me very nervous. I just happened to remember that Williams was one of the greatest left-handed distance and pull hitters of all time, and that I was in right field and didn't even know how to adjust my sunglasses. After all, it was only a couple of weeks earlier, in a game at Phoenix, that a fly ball bounced right off my head because I couldn't properly flip off the glasses.

"Cliff Mapes told me how to play Ted. 'Just back up right to the fence,' said Cliff, 'and set yourself for line drives, sinkers, and ordinary fly balls that seem to carry and carry. Those are home runs.' I was sorry that Cliff gave me that information because it only added to my being scared.

"Luckily for me, Williams singled to center, flied to left, then walked and hit a home run. Walt Dropo hit a high fly, and I was able to get it easily. Jerry Coleman cheered me up with an 'Attaboy' after I caught the ball, and I smiled back at him. After that I was a bit more settled, if you can call my knees knocking every two seconds.

"I wound up with four putouts. Caught two balls from the bat of Vern Stephens, and then I caught two more fly balls off Bobby Doerr in the eighth and ninth innings. By that time, Vic Raschi was pitching a nifty six-hitter, and we were out in front by 5–0.

Mickey Mantle and Jackie Jensen were two of the "bright prospects" invited to Casey Stengel's prespring training instructional schools for Yankee rookies.

"I must tell you folks about my first big-league hit. It was a long time coming. I thought so, anyway.

"Bobby Doerr threw me out in the first inning after my bat broke. I popped to Stephens in the third inning, but in the sixth inning I got a pretty solid hit. Jackie Jensen opened the inning with a double and took third on Rizzuto's scratch infield hit. Then there I was in the box again batting right-handed, and I hit Wight's first pitch for a sharp single that scored Jensen, and I became a happy player for a day.

"I was even happier the next day when I got a two-run single off Harry Taylor in a four-run fifth inning. Ed Lopat had one of his great days and pitched a two-hitter, and we won 6–3.

"The third day I began to learn the facts of big-league baseball. The Yankees also could lose, and we did just that in Washington. Worse yet, I showed up my number one weakness, by striking out twice, and that was only the beginning of my worries.

"I had averaged a strikeout per game during the first five games and began to press. I was also aware that the American League pitchers had a big edge on the kind of pitching I had been seeing at Joplin. I got lucky against the Athletics and got three for five against a tough pitcher—Lou Brissie—and Hank Wyse. And my average jumped to .340.

"But this time I started to get real chummy with some of the other players as we got ready for our first western trip. Frankly, I wanted to get into those hearts games that most of the players played all the time. Finally I got into a game and beat some of the guys at first.

"One day I noticed that Rizzuto had trouble getting up a foursome. So I politely asked Phil if he could use me in an emergency. Phil, always kidding, cut me down quickly.

"'I like your nerve!' screamed Rizzuto. 'The idea of a busher like you asking me about a game. Son, you've got a lot to learn. Come back in a couple of years and I might consider letting you sit next to me. And besides, you're still a minor. You'll have to ask your father.'

"But then my troubles began. I dropped to .222 before I hit my first big-league homer. It was in Chicago, May 1, off Randy Gumpert. And it was a pretty good shot—some of the players said it was my longest drive ever. The news reports said the ball traveled about 450 feet.

"I ran into my first 'trouble' with Red Patterson, the Yankees' traveling secretary. On this trip, I forgot to pack my bag and leave it in the lobby for collection on getaway day. So when I found myself heading for the train depot and St. Louis, I told Red about my suitcase, which was still in the hotel room.

"Red hit the roof. But he delivered. He grabbed a cab, rushed to the DelPardo Hotel, had the cab wait for him, rushed to the room, got the bag, and arrived back at the station a minute before the train pulled out. He forgave me after warning me never to let that happen again.

"On the field I was still striking out. But Casey continued to go along with me, although he didn't like the idea of risking me for a full nine innings as a fielder in winning ball games. Meanwhile, Casey worked with me on my throwing and had me lifting my leg like a pitcher when I threw a ball.

"I managed to hang in at about the .300 mark until late May. But I kept striking out, and my average once again began to sink.

"That was enough for Casey. He called me into his hotel room after a bad series against Cleveland. 'Mickey,' said Casey, 'you're getting a little

"Mickey, you're striking out too often. We're in a tight pennant race, and I got to use someone else. I'm gonna send you to KC, where you'll play every day and get your swing back," said Casey to Mantle. "I'll bring you back in a few weeks."

nervous and tight at the plate . . . and you're swinging at too many bad pitches. One of these days you're gonna develop into one of our biggest stars. I know it for sure. But right now, we're in a tight pennant race, and things are too tense for the team and for you. A change of scenery might do you a lotta good, and I'm gonna send you to Kansas City. There you'll play every day and get your confidence back. We got a great manager there, George Selkirk, he used to play for us here, matter of fact, Selkirk took over when Babe Ruth left the Yankees. He's great with young players. He's got orders to play you in center field.'"

As for Mickey himself, he masked his disappointment as bravely as he could. "It's all right with me," he said. "I'd rather play every day with the minors than sit on the bench. Nobody has to tell me that I've got plenty to learn about playing the outfield and about hitting."

Mickey left the Yankees in Detroit and joined Kansas City, then in the Class AAA American Association, in Milwaukee. In his first time at bat for KC, Mickey beat out a bunt and reached first base safely. But after he scored a run, Selkirk took him aside. "Look, Mickey, you're not here to bunt. When I want you to bunt, I'll tell you. You're here to get your batting eye back and build up your confidence. Now let's see some of those long drives."

Mickey's next nineteen times at bat were fruitless. He was unable to get a single base hit, and he returned with the team in Kansas City in a grave personal crisis, "the worst time of my life," he later admitted. But there was help coming for Mantle.

Mutt Mantle had read all the stories about Mickey's problems and told his wife, "I'm going to take a couple of days off and go see what the problem is with Mickey. Maybe I can help."

Mutt came to Kansas City and confronted Mickey.

He listened while Mickey sobbed out his story. "I'm just not cut out for big-league ball. Maybe I just ought to quit the whole thing now."

Mutt looked his boy squarely in the eye.

"If that's all the guts you got, why just pack up and come home to Commerce. There you'll get your job back as a miner, and someday you'll be as old and tired as I am at forty years of age. Now, look at what you've already done, Mickey. You made the Yankees and you got more money than any rookie, and you paid the mortgage on our home. Baseball is like another tough job. Things get rough, but you've got to learn to take the bad with the good. And the sooner, the better. Now, let's see you get out there and play the kind of ball that I know you can."

"I'm sorry, Dad," Mickey said.

Mutt Mantle smiled and promised that he would come to Kansas City as often as he could and bring up the family to see Mickey play ball.

The next day, a determined Mickey Mantle drove out a base hit. The following day he slugged out a home run and a double. In a game at

Columbus, late in July, Mickey delivered a triple, two home runs, and a single, and by August, a renewed Mantle had appeared in 40 games for KC. His batting average was one of the top ten in the league with a potent .361 average, including 11 home runs, and with 60 base hits.

And the Yankees, now in a desperate race with the Cleveland Indians, called Mickey back to rejoin the team in Cleveland.

But before he could rejoin the Yankees, Mickey received another call. The Army wanted to examine him once again. He flew to Fort Sill, Oklahoma, where six doctors, including a couple of orthopedic specialists, put him under a complete examination. An Army spokesman explained, "Mantle's receiving an unusually thorough examination so there will be no doubt as to his condition, and whether he is eligible to serve."

Then came the good news for Mickey. All six doctors verified that Mickey was still suffering from osteomyelitis. They all agreed that Mickey was "unacceptable by present Army standards."

Then Mickey was on his way to Cleveland to rejoin the Yankees. The day after he rejoined the team, Mantle was back in the starting lineup. And he slugged a 2-run homer off the slants of Mike Garcia as the Yankees whipped Cleveland, 7–3. A week later, with the entire Mantle clan present in St. Louis, Mickey drove in 4 runs with a home run and a single as the Yankees continued their battle for the top post in the league.

Waiting word from his draft board in 1951, Mickey Mantle drinks a few glasses of milk as his mother pours. Mantle was at home in Oklahoma. A few days later he was informed that he was 4-F because of his osteomyelitis.

One weekend in August, with all the Mantles again enjoying box seats at Yankee Stadium, Mickey came up to bat against the crafty Bob Porterfield of the Senators. Porterfield and Ed Lopat were locked in a tight pitchers' duel, with the score 0–0. Porterfield walked one man and then walked another batter, and with two men on base, Mantle came up to hit. Porterfield got set and hurled a sizzling fastball across the plate. Mickey timed the pitch and smashed a screaming line drive that kept going, going, going until it cleared the wall of the right-field bleachers. It was a drive of more than 425 feet, and the Yankees went on to win the game, 4–0.

The next day Mantle again hit a long drive for another home run against the Senators as part of a doubleheader. In the second game Mickey also drove in the winning run, and the Yankees were able to pull out a shortened five-inning game, 2–0, after a deluge of rain swamped the field.

In a vital series against Cleveland, late in the season, Mickey slashed out a home run, two triples, and two doubles in three games that virtually clinched the pennant for the Yankees.

8

MANTLE'S FIRST WORLD SERIES

Now it was the Yankees facing the New York Giants, who had produced a miracle victory when outfielder Bobby Thomson cracked a home run against the Dodgers in the final league play-off game to virtually grab the pennant from the Dodgers.

It had been fourteen years since the Yankees and the Giants had met in a World Series, and all of New York City was jumping with excitement.

In the opening game the Giants, still red hot, won behind the superb pitching of Dave Koslo, who beat Allie Reynolds, 5–1. Mickey as well as most of the other Yankees went hitless in this game.

The next day the Giants pitched Larry Jansen, and Mickey, leading off in the first inning, dragged a bunt single, his first World Series hit. In the third inning he struck out.

In the top of the fifth, Willie Mays came to bat for the Giants. Mantle was shaded toward right-center, figuring Mays to pull the ball. Willie got ahold of a fast ball and lifted a high fly that headed between Mantle and Joe DiMaggio. Mickey shot over toward the ball, then heard DiMaggio call for it. At that instant, Mickey felt something pop in his knee. Suddenly he fell in a heap. He pitched over on his face and lay motionless on the ground.

DiMaggio made the catch of Mays's fly ball, then quickly bent down

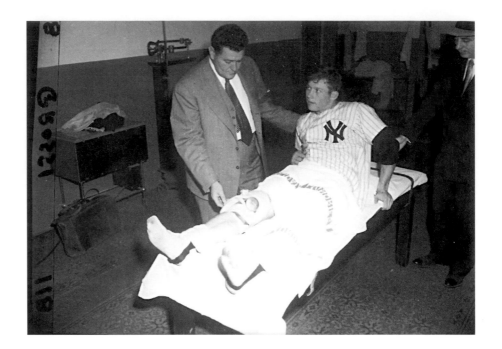

Dr. Sydney Gaynor checks Mickey Mantle's knee in the dressing room at Yankee Stadium after Mickey injured himself chasing a fly ball in the fifth inning of the second World Series game, Oct. 5, 1951.

over Mickey. "What's the matter, kid?" he asked. Mickey was too frightened to answer.

They carried him off the field on a stretcher. Then Dr. Sidney Gaynor, the Yankee physician, packed the knee in ice and wrapped a stiff elastic bandage around it.

Newsmen crowded in on Mickey after the game, which the Yankees won, 3–1. By now Mantle had regained some of his composure. But he wouldn't give any reason for falling.

"One minute I was driving after the ball, and the next moment, the knee gave out. I fell and stayed on the ground as the knee pained like hell. I thought I'd broken my kneecap or something."

Mutt Mantle hurried to the Yankee clubhouse, greatly concerned about his son. He drove in a cab with Mickey to Lenox Hill Hospital. As Mutt tried to help Mickey out of the cab, the father suddenly collapsed to the street.

And so it was that Mickey watched the rest of the World Series on television, with his right leg propped up. Dr. Gaynor's diagnosis: a torn ligament on the inner side of the leg. In the bed next to Mickey's, his father lay gravely ill.

Mickey's first year in the major leagues was over, and he brought home a sizable World Series check plus his regular salary. But he also brought home the dreadful news that his beloved Mutt Mantle had Hodgkin's disease and was slowly dying.

"Dad and I stuck around the hospital for another week. Dr. Gaynor braced my knee with a heavy bandage and told me to take it nice and easy," said Mickey. "Then after checking and rechecking the knee, Dad and I headed back to Commerce.

"I tried to rest and limp around on crutches, then Dad thought we ought to go to the Mayo Clinic in Rochester, Minnesota, for further treatment. The Mayo Clinic doctors gave me some weights to lift with my right knee, to exercise and strengthen the knee, and I worked with them for a couple of weeks. Then after a couple of weeks I stopped.

"I started to play some football, and kicked the ball quite a bit, but it was a mistake, and the pain was there all the time."

For quite some time, Mickey wore a special brace, plus a weighted boot. He and a couple of friends spent much of the winter tramping around the woods hunting for squirrels and quail. Now Mickey was doing something he loved, for hunting was almost second nature for any teenage boy in that part of northeastern Oklahoma.

One of the first things Mickey did upon returning home to Commerce after the 1951 World Series was to visit with his brothers Ray (L) and Roy. Both Mantle boys were stars of Commerce High School's football team.

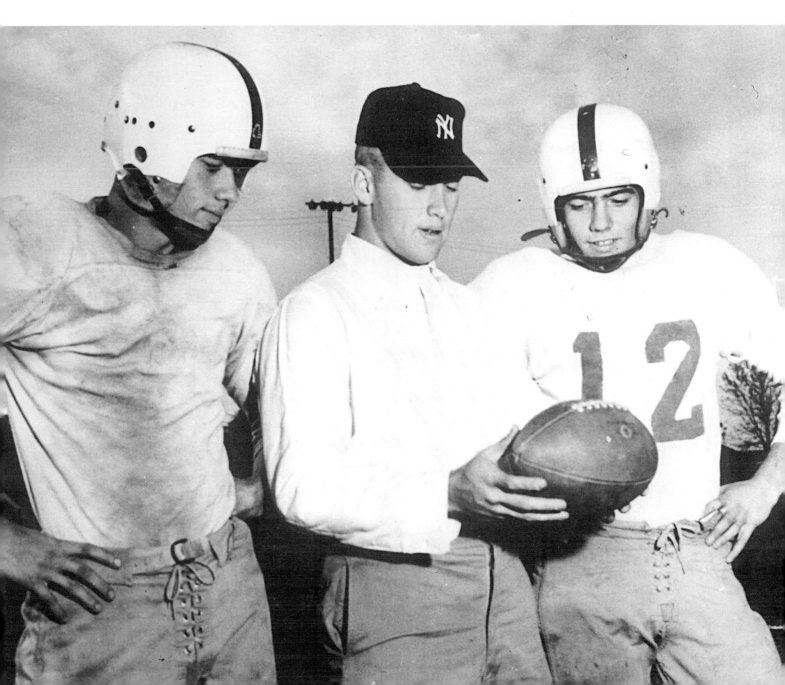

9

A NEW CENTER FIELDER

On December 11, 1951, came a startling announcement out of New York that was headline news on sports pages throughout the nation. After thirteen seasons as a Yankee, thirteen years in which the Yankees won ten pennants and nine World Championships, Joe DiMaggio announced he was retiring. At the same time, Casey Stengel told the press that he fully expected that Mickey Mantle would take over Joe's old position in center field.

Mickey was flattered by Stengel's report, then said, "It was great hearing that Casey had such confidence in me, but I want to say that it would be impossible for any player to take Joe's place. But they can count on me doing the very best I can. That I promise.

"Right now, I'm looking forward to seeing a lot of my girlfriend, Merlyn, having some fun watching my twin brothers, Ray and Roy, play football with Commerce High School, and doing some hunting and fishing."

But Mickey was concerned. "All this time I kept worrying about my bad knee as it kept hurting. It just kept hurting every time I put some pressure on it. And what bothered me," said Mickey, "I never had experienced the slightest kind of problem with my knees until I had that accident in the 1951 World Series.

"I thought a lot about DiMaggio, and thinking about him eased some of my own problems. As everyone knows, Joe started out with the Yankees as a gamble in 1936, because he had a bad knee. Even though he had just hit .398 with San Francisco in the Pacific Coast League, few teams wanted to make a deal for Joe.

"And, of course, I knew all about Joe's operations for the removal of bone spurs on his heels, starting in 1947. I secretly hoped that I would be able to shake off my injuries as Joe finally did," said Mickey.

"Most of the Yankee stars, past and present, were broken up somewhere along the line. Rizzuto was badly spiked his first year at Bassets in the Tri-State League and almost lost a leg as a result. That was in 1937. Tommy Henrich had more injuries than I could count. Hank Bauer had fought with the Marines at Okinawa in World War II. Ralph Houk served with the Rangers and was a real hero. Jerry Coleman piloted a dive bomber for the Marines in World War II and Korea, and Johnny Mize had all kinds of injuries.

"I didn't have to tell Casey about my aching knee. He saw me limp during the first practices in 1952, and he told me to take it easy. My so-called running never fooled Casey. He'd take a look at me running and would yell at me to go easy. So he just used me as a pinch hitter when the exhibition games started. I pinch hit and guys would run for me when I got a hit. I played in the outfield—alternating in at right and left field, with Jackie Jensen in center field.

"On March 18 at St. Petersburg, we played the Braves, and I replaced Archie Wilson in the fifth inning. The Braves beat us in a great 1–0 game in the fourteenth inning. Those last nine innings encouraged me that my knee was slowly coming around. The next day, against the Phillies in Clearwater, I was in right field and hit a single and home run as we lost, 8–1.

"I opened the season against the Athletics in right field. Jensen played center and Hank Bauer was in left, and I felt great for the first time as we won, 8–1. Vic Raschi allowed the A's just five hits for the win. I made four putouts in the field and got three hits, including a two-run double.

"Throughout April I remained in right field as Jensen, Gene Woodling, and Bob Cerv alternated in center. Then the Yankees pulled a 'big trade' with the Senators as Jackie Jensen, Spec Shea, and Wilson went to Washington for Irv Noren, a solid-hitting center fielder.

"Then, on May 6, 1952, Dad died in a Denver hospital.

"Although I—the whole family—had known for some months that Dad's passing would be only a matter of time, his death left me with a terrible lonesomeness. I had the feeling of being a little boy again, his hand reaching out to lead me to ball games and teaching and preaching baseball to me as far back as I can remember. Somehow, though, the hand was still there, and kids who grew up with fathers as I did know what I am trying to say.

"The Cleveland Indians were at the Stadium when I got the news. A night game was scheduled and I knew Dad would have wanted me to play. The players were great to me, and Casey was particularly understanding. He wanted to know if I had gotten in touch with my mother because there had been some trouble getting through to Commerce on the phone.

"Casey told me not to return until I was good and ready. He then cheered me up, actually making me grin by cracking something about needing me something awful. Casey wasn't kidding me, though. The Sunday before, in a doubleheader, I had gone one-for-nine, and my batting average dropped to .250."

Mickey went back to Commerce for the funeral, and fighting back the tears, he began to realize that he was now the man of the family. Now it was up to him to support his dad's family as well as his own. "Baseball had been a game before Dad died," Mickey said. "After his death it became a profession. I had to make it, and make it worthwhile."

"I was back in the Stadium on May 11 against the Red Sox. In the outfield there was Bauer, Noren, and me. My knee, almost by magic, began to feel better.

"Then, on May 20, Billy Martin signaled me that I was not only in the lineup, but I was in center field and batting third. And I felt great and got my first four-hit game of the year. I got two singles off Ken Holcombe and two singles off Chuck Stobbs as Johnny Sain pitched a six-hitter, and we won the game, 3–1.

"I kept hitting the ball, and by June 3 I was hitting .333, thanks to another four-hit day against Billy Pierce of the White Sox, and we took a 4–3 game.

"I knew I had to keep hitting to remain in center field. Luckily, I stayed there even though I slumped to .290. But on June 21, I pulled back over .300 and managed to finish the season with a pretty good .311 average."

For the remainder of the season Mantle along with pitcher Allie Reynolds, were the two most valuable members of the team.

In an important game at Detroit, Mickey smashed a gigantic home run that measured nearly 450 feet. The homer won the game.

On July 13, in one of the most memorable games of the year, Mickey slashed a home run against the Tigers, batting left-handed. Then, in the second game of the doubleheader, Mick, batting right-handed against the great Hal Newhouser, drove out another home run. Both home runs aided the Yankee cause as they took two games from the Tigers.

On September 2, the Yankees continued their torrid play as Ewell Blackwell and Johnny Sain shut out the Red Sox for a brilliant 2–0 win and moved to the top of the American League by 3½ games.

But three days later, the Athletics beat the Yanks to cut their margin to 2½ games. Two days later, in a doubleheader, Mize and Mantle homered in both games as the Yankees beat the Senators, 5–2 and 5–3.

The Yanks lost a couple of games. Then, on September 11, leading Cleveland by half a game, they charged into Cleveland, and in front of a frenzied Indians crowd of 73,000 fans and with Mantle hammering out a double, single, and home run, they beat the Indians to give them a 1½-game edge.

In a game Boston fans will never forget, Mantle doubled in the first of a twin bill; then his triple gave the Yankees a 10th-inning victory. In the second game, Mick singled, then tripled, and to cap things off, hit a home run as the Yankees won both games.

Two days later, on September 26, in Philadelphia, the Yanks and the A's were tied at 2–2, when Mantle smashed a home run with two men on to give them a 5–2 win in a historic game that clinched the pennant for New York.

In the clubhouse after the victorious game, Stengel led the team in a wild celebration that featured all the champagne one could drink—a celebration that carried on until the early hours of the morning.

And the rookie, Mickey Mantle, playing his first full season with the World Champions, had done more than his share in the drive for the team's fourth straight title. Over the season, Mantle had driven out 37 doubles, seven triples, and 23 home runs, with a solid .311 batting average.

Casey Stengel summed up the season with just one paragraph: "That youngster Mantle, not twenty years old, and still wet behind the ears, was the reason. He picked up this team when we were down and nearly out, and his speed and his big bat brought us back to win. Just like Joe DiMaggio did the last couple of years."

On September 11, 1952, the Yankees came into Cleveland Stadium just half a game behind the league-leading Indians. In the battle for first place, Mantle first hit a single, later a double, then a gigantic home run to beat the Indians. Yogi Berra, in photo, is shown congratulating Mickey after his home run.

The 1952 Dodgers won the National League pennant over the Giants by 6 1/2 games and then came within a game of defeating the Yankees in the World Series. Here are the Dodgers after winning the pennant. Manager Chuck Dressen (center) leads his team in a rip-roaring celebration.

In the first game of the 1952 World Series, played at Ebbets Field, Duke Snider caught a fastball by Allie Reynolds with Pee Wee Reese on base and slammed a long home run over the center field fence to win the game for the Dodgers by a 4-2 score. Photo shows the Yankee players in the field and the flight of Snider's drive.

But the season wasn't really over yet. There was still a rough-and-tumble World Series against the great Brooklyn Dodgers, and it was anybody's guess who would win.

In the 1952 World Series the Dodgers were out for blood. Three years earlier they had battled Casey Stengel's Yankees and had taken a humiliating beating, four games to one.

But this was a different Dodger nine. They were a hard-hitting, fast-moving, smart ball club with such stars as Jackie Robinson, Pee Wee Reese, Don Newcombe, Joe Black, Duke Snider, Carl Furillo, Roy Campanella, Gil Hodges, Carl Erskine, Billy Loes, Preacher Roe, and their manager Chuck Dressen, who was considered one of the brainiest managers in the National League.

Casey Stengel addressed his team in the clubhouse before the first game and said, "Don't go kiddin' yourselves about these here Dodgers. Look who they got. Robinson who can hit and run those bases like a jackrabbit. Then Duke Snider, Hodges. Why, that Hodges is so strong, when he hits the ball, it just vanishes. And Campanella and Furillo, they're pretty good, and they got great pitching, and they run like greyhounds at the track. Now, you all got to keep your thinking caps on all the time against this team."

In the first game, at Ebbets Field, the Dodgers won, 4–2, behind a home run by Duke Snider off Allie Reynolds with Reese on base. Mantle got two hits, both singles.

In the second game, Vic Raschi was unbeatable as he held the Brooks to just three hits. Billy Martin drove hit a home run with two on as the Yankees knocked out Erskine in the fifth inning.

The Dodgers came back in the third game, at Yankee Stadium, for a

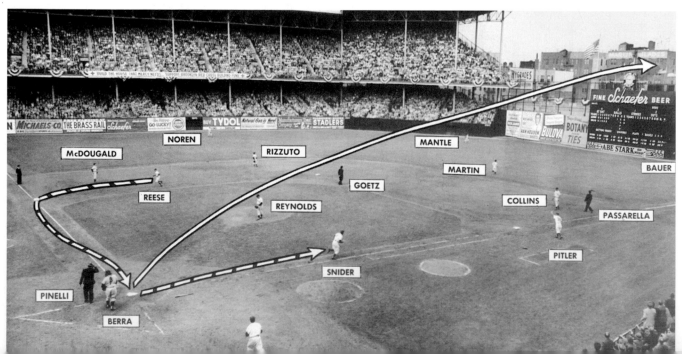

Left: The Yankees' Vic Raschi (left) and the Dodgers' Carl Erskine compare grips before the second game of the Dodger-Yankee World Series. Raschi, who posted a 16-6 record during the regular season, won the game, 7-1. Raschi also won the sixth game, 3-2, in a close battle with Billy Loes.

Below: The Dodger left fielder, Andy Pafko, became an instant Ebbets Field hero in the second inning of the fifth game of the 1952 World Series at Yankee Stadium as he leaped high into the air to rob a home run from the Yankees' Gene Woodling. The Dodgers won the game, 6-5.

5–3 win as Preacher Roe outpitched Ed Lopat for the win.

In the fourth game, the Yankees found they were in a war. Allie Reynolds came back to battle Joe Black and was masterful as he outpitched the Dodger ace and the Yankees won, 2–0, Mize homered and Mantle tripled and scored a run and was responsible for the second run in an exciting game that went to the wire.

In the fifth game, Carl Erskine had a 4–0 lead going into the fifth inning. Then all of a sudden he was battered for five runs, and the Yanks had a 5–4 lead. Then the Dodgers tied the game and won it in the eleventh inning on a single by Duke Snider.

For six innings of the sixth game Vic Raschi and Billy Loes were invincible. But in the last of the sixth, Duke Snider blasted a home run, and the Dodgers had a one-run edge. In the top of the seventh, Yogi Berra hit a long home run. Then Gene Woodling singled, advanced to second, and scored when Raschi singled to give the Yankees a 2–1 edge.

In the top of the eighth inning, with the big crowd in a frenzy, Mickey Mantle came up to hit, and on Billy Loes's first pitch, drove the ball out of the ballpark. It was a clincher, and when Mickey returned to the Yankee dugout, the entire team came out to greet him. Now the Series was tied, 3–3.

The Dodgers started their ace, Joe Black, in the Series-deciding seventh game, while Casey sent Ed Lopat to the hill for the Yankees. For three innings it was a scoreless pitching duel. In the fourth inning, both teams scored a run. Then in the sixth inning Mantle came up to hit, picked out a Joe Black fastball, and drove it out of the ballpark, and the Yankees led, 3–2. An inning later, Mantle singled off Roe to drive another run to make it 4–2 for the Yankees.

The Dodgers' half of the inning was a thriller. With one out and the bases loaded, Kuzava got Snider on a pop fly. Then with everybody running, Jackie Robinson hits another pop fly that looked easy to catch. But a high wind caught the ball and blew it away. Everybody froze and just looked at the ball. Then suddenly Billy Martin tore in and just managed to get the ball a couple of feet off the ground. It was the big play of the game, and the Yankees took the game and another World Series.

In the biggest play of the 1952 World Series, Billy Martin, the Yanks' second baseman, makes a diving one-hand catch of a Jackie Robinson pop fly that ended a Dodger rally and won the game for the Yanks.

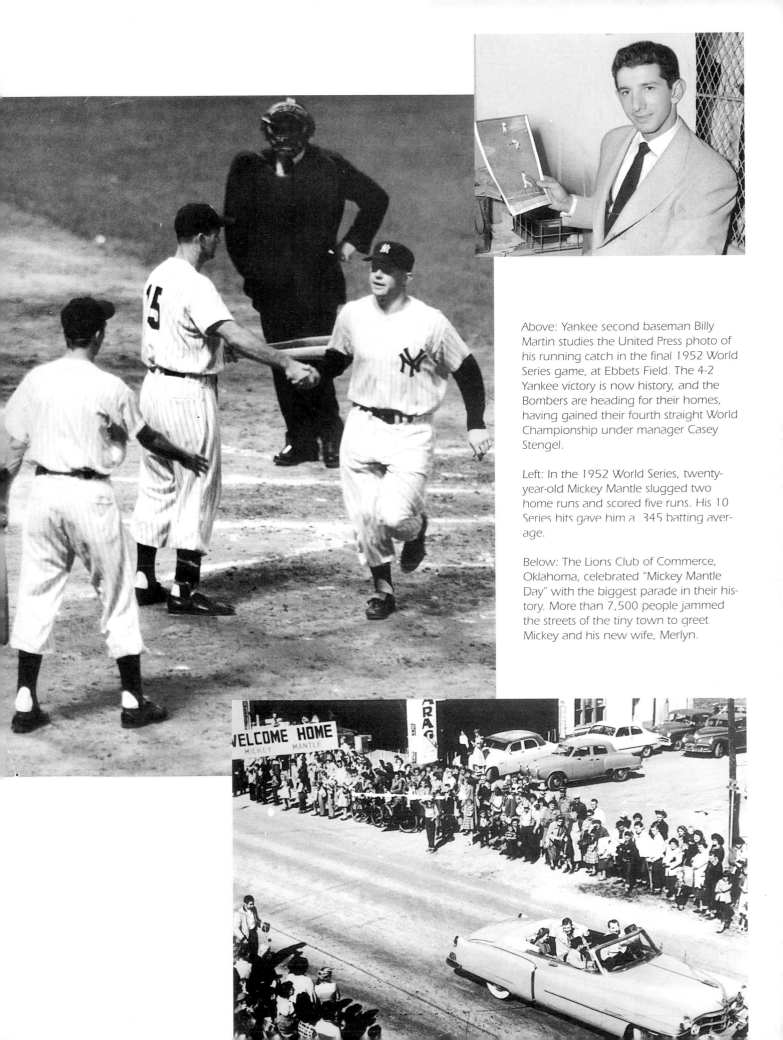

Above: Yankee second baseman Billy Martin studies the United Press photo of his running catch in the final 1952 World Series game, at Ebbets Field. The 4-2 Yankee victory is now history, and the Bombers are heading for their homes, having gained their fourth straight World Championship under manager Casey Stengel.

Left: In the 1952 World Series, twenty-year-old Mickey Mantle slugged two home runs and scored five runs. His 10 Series hits gave him a .345 batting average.

Below: The Lions Club of Commerce, Oklahoma, celebrated "Mickey Mantle Day" with the biggest parade in their history. More than 7,500 people jammed the streets of the tiny town to greet Mickey and his new wife, Merlyn.

The Yankees were World Champions for the fourth straight season, and twenty-year-old Mickey Mantle was the hero of the Series.

In the seven-game 1952 World Series, Mantle batted .345. He drove out 10 hits, including two home runs, a triple, and a double. He scored five runs and handled sixteen outfield chances without an error, and when Mickey and his new wife, Merlyn, and mother returned to Commerce after the Series ended, the Lions Club and a number of outstanding citizens organized a Mickey Mantle Day in Commerce.

Schoolchildren got the entire day off. An outstanding football game between Oklahoma and Eastern Oklahoma was moved to Commerce for the occasion. The entire Main Street of Commerce was decorated in flags and bunting, and there were sixteen bands for the big parade that was to climax Mickey Mantle Day.

A crowd estimated at more than 7,500 packed Main Street to pay tribute to Mickey and Merlyn as they sat on the backseat of a Cadillac and took the applause and the salutes of the well-wishers.

The great day for Mickey came to a close with a dinner, and various speakers talked about Mantle and how much he meant to Commerce. Tom Greenwade, the Yankee scout who discovered Mantle; pitching star Allie Reynolds; and the mayor of Commerce also spoke about Mantle's virtues.

Finally Mickey got up to address the banquet and said simply, "Many thanks to everybody for making this day such a great day for Commerce and for me and my family.

"Later that night, after all the festivities," said Mickey, "I jumped into the car and drove out to the GAR cemetery, where Dad was buried. I snapped off all the lights and thought about how it all began. . . . from the switch-hitting of tennis balls to the Pee Wee League . . . then high school ball . . . the terrible situation with that kick in my shin playing football, and then osteomyelitis, Greenwade and the Yankee contract . . . Independence and Joplin . . . 1951, my rookie year with the Yankees at Phoenix and my start in the big leagues. . . . a dream come true. My demotion to Kansas City and back to the Yankees to stay. My injury in the 1951 World Series and being together in the same hospital room with Dad . . . and his death.

"The grass covering Dad's grave was fresh and unusually bright green, I thought, for the middle of October. And I don't believe I ever saw the moon shining more brightly."

In February 1945, the Yankees were sold for the second time in their history. The purchasers were Larry MacPhail, baseball's dynamic redhead who had wrought wonders with his promotions in Cincinnati and in Brooklyn; Dan Topping, heir to tin plate millions and still on duty in the South Pacific as a Marine captain; and Del Webb, a former minor-league pitcher and owner of a multimillion-dollar construction company in Phoenix. The price was reported to be $2.8 million, which included not only the Yankees but also Yankee Stadium, the Newark Bears, the Kansas City Blues, and other clubs in their minor-league chain.

In 1946 MacPhail sold his interest to Webb and Topping and retired to his horse farm in Maryland. The Yankees, under the direction of Webb, Topping, and Ed Barrow, and George Weiss handling the overall direction of the team, had hired Bucky Harris to manage the club in 1947.

The easygoing Harris, who loved horse racing almost as much as baseball, spent a good deal of time at the track, and that dismayed Weiss so much that even though the Yankees won a World Championship in 1947 and came in a close third in the 1948 American League pennant race, Weiss fired him, and the Yankees began a search for a new manager.

Late in 1948, after Ed Barrow left the Yankees, George Weiss brought up the name of Casey Stengel as the next manager. Dan Topping didn't particularly care for Stengel, but Del Webb convinced Topping. "My sole contribution to the Yankees," said Webb, "was in signing Casey Stengel as manager."

Webb told noted sportswriter Frank Graham, "I got to know Stengel when he was managing Oakland. He won there and developed a number of pretty good ballplayers. He managed the Dodgers, Braves, and played ball for more than twenty years and had established a sound reputation as a player, coach, and manager, as well as a raffish reputation as a 'clown.'"

Below left: Bucky Harris managed the Washington Senators to the World Series in 1924 and 1925 and was named Yankee manager in 1947. Under Harris the Yankees won the Series in 1947, and finished in third place in 1948. But Yankee general manager George Weiss did not like Harris's great interest in horse racing. "He was at the track too much," said Weiss, and in 1949 Harris was fired and the Yankees had a new manager.

Below right: Early in 1949, Del Webb, the new Yankee owner along with Dan Topping, suggested that the Yanks hire Casey Stengel as the new manager.

At a press conference at New York's famous 21 Club, Casey was nervous, quiet, and subdued. Following Charlie Grimm in Milwaukee might have been the toughest job he'd ever had. But that was nothing compared to managing the Yankees. Most of the sportswriters at the press conference thought well of Stengel, but they thought his hiring was more of a public relations ploy, a move to divert attention from the curt dismissal of Bucky Harris. Harris was popular, and the writers were unhappy with his firing.

But Casey in rebuttal said, "The Yankees are big business. I didn't get this job because of friendship with Mr. Webb. They don't hand out jobs like this because they like your company. I got the job here with the Yankees because the people here think I can produce for them."

Sometime later the photographers put him in a Yankee uniform and a Yankee cap, and they posed him behind a backlighted baseball with an exaggerated look of wonder on his face, as though he were gazing into a crystal ball. The photo was widely circulated and received an impressive response, not all of it to Casey's credit. A member of the Yanks' front office winced when he saw it. "We have hired a clown," he wailed.

In Boston, sportswriter Dave Egan, who had battled and feuded with Casey through the years he managed the Braves, got out his typewriter and wrote, "Well, ladies and gents, the Yankees have now mathematically eliminated themselves from the 1949 pennant race when they engaged Perfessor Stengel to mismanage them for the next two years, and you may be sure that the perfessor will oblige to the best of his unique ability."

Stengel had spent almost forty years in baseball, and it was as though he had done nothing of value. He still had to prove himself. He was almost fifty-nine years old, an age when most men are looking for-

A veteran campaigner and an old hand at victory parties, Casey Stengel laughs heartily while rookie left hander Whitey Ford has eyes only for his bride-to-be, Joan Foran. Earlier in the day Ford had pitched and won over the Phillies to clinch the 1950 World Series for the Yankees in four straight games.

Casey Stengel is absolutely speechless as he eyes his second baseman,
Billy Martin, dressed in the costume
he wore to entertain guests at a
1952 spring training party.

ward to retirement, and he was taking on the biggest challenge of his life.

During spring training in 1949, Casey's first as manager of the Yankees, Joe DiMaggio was in a quiet corner of the Yankee clubhouse one day talking with Arthur Daley of *The New York Times*.

"What do you think of our new manager?" DiMaggio asked.

"I never saw such a bewildered guy in my life," Daley replied. "He doesn't seem to know what this is all about."

"That's the impression I have," said DiMaggio, "and the rest of the fellows feel the same."

But under Stengel's direction, shifting players in and out, penciling in a different lineup almost every day, the Yankees took a thrilling 5–3 win over the Red Sox to win the pennant on the final day of the regular season and then defeated the Brooklyn Dodgers in the World Series.

In the celebration that followed, Stengel said, "I want to thank all these Yankee players for giving me the greatest thrill of my life." To his death, it remained his greatest thrill.

Casey won it all again in 1950 with a changing cast of Yankee faces, Johnny Mize, Charlie Keller, Tommy Henrich, Johnny Lindell, and with DiMaggio hitting at a .370 clip towards the end of the year, the Yankees won another pennant. In the World Series the Yankees demolished the Philadelphia Phillies Whiz Kids in four games.

Now in 1951, the Yankees, under Stengel, shifted their spring training base to Phoenix to please Del Webb, who wanted to show off his team to friends there.

In Phoenix Stengel assembled some forty of their brightest young minor-league stars in a two to three-week preseason camp—"an instructional school," Casey called it. Three of the brightest stars were Mickey Mantle, Gil McDougald, and Tom Morgan.

In 1951 Stengel boasted, "Everybody thought ol' Case was a joke when the Yankees brought me in, and everybody thought it was a joke when ol' Case set up those instructional schools. Now everybody is copying the schools. Only we're three years ahead of them."

Mickey Mantle was the nugget, the prize of the school.

Tom Greenwade, the Yankee scout who had discovered Mickey and signed him, told a sportswriter, "I don't know how to put it, but what I'm trying to say is the first time I saw Mantle I knew how Paul Krichell felt when he first scouted Lou Gehrig. He knew that as a scout he'd never have another moment like it. I feel the same way about Mantle."

The regular season began, and nearly all the sportswriters picked the Cleveland Indians to win it all. And they had good reason for picking the Indians, for the Yankees stars were getting older.

DiMaggio wasn't DiMaggio any longer. The great relief pitcher Joe Page was gone. Whitey Ford was in the Army. First base was a mess, with Tommy Henrich retired and Johnny Mize at thirty-eight years of age attempting to handle that post.

So Stengel used his rookies. He had Mantle in right field, and Jackie Jensen in center when DiMaggio didn't feel well. Stengel put McDougald at third base and moved Tom Morgan into a starting pitcher's role.

"He took chances with those kids of his," said Cleveland's great manager Al Lopez. "He'd stick with a kid, nurse

In 1951 Casey Stengel brought the brightest stars of his "instructional camp" to New York, and they became members of the Yankee team. (L-R) Gil McDougald, Tom Morgan, and Mickey Mantle are shown at Yankee Stadium before a game.

him. Casey would sit and talk with the kid for hours, and his patience paid off and he won the pennant and another World Series."

"We did it! We did it!" shouted Stengel. He knew what he had done, and it was more than winning a World Series. He had won three pennants and three World Series in a row. Now, if he could win the pennant again in 1953, he would tie John McGraw's string of four straight set in the 1920s. A decade later, Joe McCarthy had managed the Yankees to four consecutive World Championships. One more pennant and one more World Series would tie McCarthy's great record. It was no longer a matter of proving he could manage.

He had to prove he was best of 'em all.

As the 1953 season got under way, the Yankees, starting slowly but with Gene Woodling and Mantle slugging the ball, started to pull away from the other teams—all except the Cleveland Indians, who were in first place.

Then on April 24, the Yanks defeated the St. Louis Browns in a

In 1953 the Yankees started the season slowly and the Indians pulled out to a big first-place lead. But ever so slowly, the Yankee big bats, Mantle, Berra, Hank Bauer, Joe Collins, and Gene Woodling, began to produce victories. By June 5 they were in first place. (L-R) Yogi Berra, Mantle, Joe Collins, Hank Bauer, and Gene Woodling — all kneeling.

scorcher as Mickey hit another long shot, blasting the ball 484 feet for a tremendous homer to win the game in the tenth inning. This win moved the Yanks into first place, and by the first week in June they had a 5½-game edge on the Indians.

Then Mantle injured his tricky right knee once again and was sidelined for several days, and the Yanks dropped nine in a row. Now the Indians were on their backs. On September 14, after Mickey had been in the lineup and with Ford and Lopat and Johnny Sain all pitching as if their lives depended on their performances, the Yankees clinched another pennant.

This triumph was a team effort. Whitey Ford won eighteen games, Ed Lopat won sixteen. Gene Woodling was the batting leader with a .306 average, Hank Bauer hit .304, Berra .296 and Mantle .295 with 21 home runs.

Once again the Yankees met the Dodgers in the World Series, and the result was the same for the Yanks. They won another World Championship. Mantle hit only .208 for the Series, but two of his hits were drives that won two games.

In the second game, against Preacher Roe, Mickey drove out a two-run homer that won the game, 4–2. In the fifth game he slugged a home

Above: The 1953 Yankee pennant was a team effort. Whitey Ford won 18 games, Mickey Mantle hit 21 home runs. And in the World Series, Billy Martin was the big star with 12 hits in 24 at-bats, including two home runs, two triples, and eight RBIs.

Right: In 1954 Billy Martin was called into the Army and Vic Raschi, one of the Yankees' top pitchers, was traded to the Cardinals. As a result, the Yankees did not perform up to par and finished eight games behind first-place Cleveland.

run off Russ Meyer, a grand slam that gave the Yanks an 11–7 win.

And for Billy Martin, he had the Series of his young life. Martin drove out 12 hits in 24 times at bat—including two home runs, two triples, and a double—scored five runs and drove in eight.

Well, there it was, five straight pennants and World Series victories for Casey Stengel. His explanation for this unbelievable achievement was simple.

"I got the players who can execute," he said.

In 1954 Stengel got the players he wanted, but they did not always execute in the way he wanted them to. There were a number of notable changes in the remarkable team he had assembled in the five years in which he won World Championships.

The first notable departure was Billy Martin, who was called back into the Army. Then Vic Raschi, one of the greatest Yankee pitchers, got into a salary hassle with George Weiss and was sold to the St. Louis Cardinals. Two players developed in the Yankee farm system were ordered to report: Bob Grim, a Brooklyn-born hurler signed by the Yanks in 1948, had pitched well on such farm clubs as Butler, Norfolk, Beaumont, and Binghamton and had just been released by the Army after two years; and hard-hitting first baseman Bill "Moose" Skowron, from the Kansas City Blues. Remaining with the club, however, were Mickey Mantle, Yogi Berra, Gil McDougald, Hank Bauer, Gene Woodling, Joe Collins, Jerry Coleman, Whitey Ford, Ed Lopat, Allie Reynolds and Phil Rizzuto.

At Cleveland, manager Al Lopez put together a team that had the best pitching staff in the league, augmented by a trio of sluggers. The Indians won a record number of games, 111, to win the pennant. Stengel, in defeat, called the Indians "a bunch of plumbers."

In the final look at the Yankees' record for the year, Bill Skowron hit .340 part-time, Irv Noren hit .319, Yogi Berra .307, Andy Carey .302 and Mickey Mantle hit for a .300 average, with a team high of 27 home runs.

But Casey was angry with Mantle all year long.

"Here was a great player, who struck out much too often because he wanted to hit a home run every time he got up to hit. He doesn't listen to me or anybody else. He does whatever he wants to and just doesn't want to help himself."

Because Mickey was Casey's own special project, Casey was never able to reach him. This was a genuine father-son relationship, but it was an angry father and a more stubborn son. Mickey was a source of constant irritation to Casey, not because he didn't become a great player, but because he didn't become the greatest player ever.

Casey wanted Mantle to become the monument that he wanted to leave behind for all to behold. But it never happened.

10

HANK BAUER, A SECOND DAD

Just before the regular season began in 1954, I got one extra break," said Mickey. "Frank Scott, who had been the Yankees' traveling secretary, was now in the business as a ballplayers' agent. He went away for a few months and left his apartment in New York City to Hank Bauer and Johnny Hopp. They asked me to share the place with them. The apartment was just across the street from one of the most popular restaurants in the city, the Stage Delicatessen. It could not have been any happier for me, for the place was right in the center of town, and my roommates, especially Hank Bauer, turned out to be one of the best things that happened to me during those early times in New York. Hank actually raised me the way no father could. He was a companion and a sympathetic friend who gave me valuable advice, like where to buy, why I shouldn't forget to tip a cabbie, and how to dodge some of the corny hazing in the clubhouse. He helped me choose my shirts, ties, and slacks, and explained to me the need of an extra suit of clothes. He advised me to get rid of my cardboard suitcase and get one that benefited a successful ballplayer on a World Championship team.

"And the Stage Delicatessen," said Mickey, "really made my life a lot easier. Like all shy people, I had a hard time going into new restaurants, not knowing whether to grab a table, afraid to order certain things. But in the Stage I was soon put at ease by Max and Hymie Asnas, owners of the

place and great baseball fans. They became good friends and I was made welcome anytime I came in, night or day.

"I also managed to brush the edges of the real nightlife of New York. The Stage was a place that collected every celebrity, and I slowly got acquainted with some of the big show business stars and I got a thrill just being there and rubbing shoulders with the likes of Red Buttons, Jack Carter, Joey Adams, Sid Caesar, Walter Winchell, Milton Berle, and that great doubletalk artist Al Kelley. As for myself, I was a hero to Max and Hymie, and I was as welcome there as at my own home.

"One thing that made life much more pleasant the first couple of years with the Yankees was the fact that I was on a team that regularly played in the World Series, and that meant an extra $7,000 to $8,000 per year at the end of the season. My first year with the Yankees I got $7,500 in salary, and the second year I got $12,000, and I made certain that the extra monies would allow me to marry Merlyn and also to pay off the mortgage on our old home. And that meant everything to me.

"When I was still a wide-eyed freshman with the Yankees I had a phone call from a man who said he was a sports agent and could help me in making hundreds of thousands of dollars in appearances and personal endorsements. He convinced me on the phone to have breakfast with him and this little guy who looked almost like a twin of the comedian Steve Allen. This fellow talked long and convincingly about all the monies that he could make for me and offered me a contract that stated we would split fifty–fifty all the money he developed with those projects. So I could hardly wait to sign the paper he submitted. We even went to his lawyer, and the lawyer okayed the deal.

"But when I told Hank Bauer about this, Hank immediately told me to call Frank Scott and have Frank look over the entire situation. I called Scott, and he said he would handle the whole thing with the Yankees' lawyer.

"At any rate, I never saw a penny from this deal, and it caused a real fuss, and I was very upset until the matter was completely settled.

"Incidentally, about six months later, Scott had me appear at some club group at Bear Mountain and I received a $5,000 check for half a day's appearance.

"From then on until I straightened out my place on the Yankees and started hitting home runs, I made no more deals and turned a deaf ear to anything resembling the same."

To many Yankee fans, the seasons of 1952 and 1953 are remembered as the years that Billy Martin emerged as a fine player and also as the years that Mickey Mantle drove out tremendous tape-measure home runs.

Martin was Stengel's boy. He had been with the Yankees off and on since 1950, but in the 1951 season he'd been sent out to Kansas City, then brought back, and after the Series had been drafted by the Army. A few months later, however, he received a hardship discharge and once again was a vital member of the Stadium cast. It all changed on April 30, 1952. Coleman was called back by the Marines for active duty in Korea. A short time later, Martin was installed at second base.

Nearly six feet tall but weighing just 165 pounds, he was twenty-two years old, tough, wiry, and brash. "The freshest busher since Durocher," veteran writers with the Yankees called him. When Billy heard it, he said:

"I wouldn't know about that. I wasn't born when Durocher was a busher. But I don't

Billy Martin, who foiled the Dodgers with his glove in the 1952 Series, just about killed them in the 1953 Series. Martin had one of the greatest World Series any player ever had as the Yankees once again took the Series from the Dodgers, this time in six games. (Photo) Stengel (R) points to spot where Martin's two home runs landed.

think I'm fresh. Cocky? Yes, I'll go for that. But just because I've had a lot of fights . . . well, I was born in a poverty-stricken neighborhood in Oakland and I had to fight ever since I can remember."

Casey was managing the Oakland club in 1946 when he first saw Martin.

"I didn't pay much attention to him," Casey said in the dugout one day. "There were a lot of kids out in a general tryout. But I looked over the kids who were bonus players. That night Red Adams, our trainer, said to me:

"'You didn't pay much attention to the best player on the field.'

"'Which one was that?' I said, and he said:

"'The kid with the big nose and ragged uniform and looks like a scarecrow. He plays on the Junior Oaks, the semipro club I manage. Can I bring him back tomorrow?'

"'Okay,'" said Casey. "'I'll look at him.' I look at this kid and I like him so much I sign him and send him to Idaho Falls. The next spring I bring him up again and I tell him he's going to Phoenix. 'You are making a big mistake, Mr. Stengel. I'm as good, maybe better than any infielder in the Coast League.' 'All right,' I said. You go out there, make good, and I'll bring you back.'

"All he does that year is to lead the League in everything and I give him a big party when the season is over and give him a big plaque for hitting .394.

"So I bring him up when I come to the Yankees and right away he's mad at me because I don't play him at second base because I have Coleman, who is the best in the league. One day I put him in there when Coleman is sick and when he sees he's hitting eighth, he says: 'Is this a joke? I suppose next time I'll be hitting behind the groundskeeper.' So he's mad at me, and he's been mad at me many times, but I think nothing of it.

"Mickey and Martin and Whitey Ford became best pals. They ran around together on the road, going to movies, eating together, and playing practical jokes on each other, both on the field and at home.

"Phil Rizzuto says that when he got together with Mickey, Ford, and Martin, Mickey forgot all of his shyness and was just as funny as anyone could be. He had that slow drawl, and such cornball sayings that you just had to bust out laughing."

"I remember one spring we were barnstorming around Texas," Rizzuto said. "Mickey and Martin had disappeared. They showed up later wearing ten-gallon hats with bullet holes in them. 'We had a gun duel,' said Mickey, straight-faced.

"During infield practice, they used to make believe they were killing each other. Mickey would reach behind his shoulder, pull out an imaginary bow and arrow, and shoot Martin. Bill would retaliate by throwing hand grenades. They were like kids," said Rizzuto.

"I would be the butt of a lot of their jokes. They knew how I hated bugs and spiders and they were always stuffing my locker with them. They even hung a stuffed mouse on the steering wheel of my car. I jumped clear out of the car at that."

The 1953 season started happily for Mantle. On April 12 an eight-pound bundle of joy in the person of a boy was born to Mickey and Merlyn. He was named Mickey Elven Mantle.

Five days later, on April 17, in one of the early games against the Senators at Griffith Stadium in Washington, the Yankees were in the lead 2–1, in the fifth inning. Berra was on first base and Chuck Stobbs was pitching for the Senators.

A raw wind cut into Stobbs's face as he got ready to pitch to Mickey Mantle. He got the sign from his catcher for the pitch to Mantle, waiting expectantly for the pitch. Stobbs wound up and fired the ball to the plate. It was a fastball over the plate. Mickey whipped his big bat behind a tremendous swing and drove the pitch high over the bleacher wall in the

In the photo below, Mantle is shown swinging left-handed with reliever Julio Moreno on the mound. Catcher is Les Peden and ump is Jim Honochick.

field. The ball cleared the wall, caromed over the football scoreboard fifty feet back, and landed on Fifth Street.

Red Patterson, the Yankees' publicity director, quickly raced out into the street and found the twelve-year-old youngster who had found the ball. Red gave the boy a couple of new balls and a $10 bill. Then Red put his tape measure to work and found that the ball hit by Mantle had traveled 565 feet. It was one of the longest home runs in the history of baseball.

In 1919 Babe Ruth hit a home run in spring training that traveled 587 feet.

Both baseballs—the one that Ruth hit and the Mantle drive—are now in the Hall of Fame at Cooperstown.

Later that season, Mantle slugged a 485-foot home run against St. Louis and a tremendous 435-foot drive in Chicago.

Casey Stengel was enthusiastic about his young slugger. "Mickey is the longest right-handed batter since Jimmie Foxx of the old Athletics and the longest left-handed slugger since Babe Ruth."

Soon every time Mantle stepped up to the plate a cry arose from the fans, "Get your tape measure!" It soon rang around the league, provoking arguments as to whether his drives were longer than those of Babe Ruth.

11

BILLY MARTIN TALKS ABOUT MANTLE

From 1950 to 1957 they were called "The Unholy Trio" by their manager, Casey Stengel. Whitey Ford, a city kid from New York; Mickey Mantle, from a tiny midwestern town; and Billy Martin, from the streets of San Francisco became the best of friends. On the field, they were a sensation. But their off-field stunts could drive a manager to the hospital.

Mickey Mantle came up to the Yankees to stay in 1951. He came up as a shortstop, the funniest shortstop I ever saw. Every once in a while he would actually catch the ball, and when he did, he'd throw it into the stands more often than not. But, oh, he could run, and he could hit that damn ball. We trained in Phoenix that year, traded camps with the Giants, and though he only weighed about 170 pounds, in batting practice he was hitting the ball over the center-field fence and batting from both sides of the plate. I never saw anything like it.

At first Mantle thought I was a fresh guy. One day Frank Crosetti was talking to me about making the double play, and I was telling Frank, "No, I was taught to do it this way." I disagreed with him, and Mickey couldn't believe I could act like that. But after a while we started palling around together and we found out that we had a lot of things in common. Neither one of us was a heavy drinker, so we'd go to the movies every day or night.

He would sit and listen to country-and-western music, and at first I didn't like the sound at all, but he got me to really sit and listen to the lyrics, and I fell in love with it.

In 1954, Ray and Roy Mantle were at Yankee Stadium going through workouts for Casey Stengel. Casey gave both boys minor-league contracts with a Yankee farm team. But after a couple of years both Mantle twins left the game. Ray was hurt and Roy went into the Army.

We'd fish and play golf together. Neither one of us was a good golfer, but we had a great time together. We'd hunt a lot.

One time we were hunting in Commerce with Mickey's twin brothers, Roy and Ray. They were big kids, almost as big as Mickey, and they could run just as fast. We were walking along this street with our guns and we walked a long distance over rows and rows of plowed dirt and then we came on a bunch of ducks sitting in a pond. Mickey and his brothers crawled around one side of the pond, and I went around the other side. We crouched down and started popping at those ducks.

After I shot, I looked up and saw Mick, Roy, and Ray running just as fast as they could back to our car. I looked around and there was this big game warden coming right toward me. It was very cold and I had layers and layers of clothing on, and as I ran, it felt like I was running in quicksand. I was hardly moving at all. I couldn't catch up with them, and here this game warden was almost on me. I wasn't about to shoot him, so I dropped to the ground and pointed my gun right at him, and when he saw that, he turned around and started running the other way. Then I got up and ran to our car and we sped away.

When I got my breath back again, I said to Mickey, "It was awful nice of you guys to warn me." And they laughed like hell.

Mickey would always be playing tricks on me. We'd go into a restaurant, and I'd see a face I recognized and I'd say to Mick, "Who's that?" He'd say, "Fred Schultz." The guy would come over to us and I'd say, "How are you, Fred?" and the guy would say, "My name's Al, Billy."

Mickey used to give me the wrong names all of time. He could remember names, and I couldn't for the life of me. But he would pull this all the time, and then would laugh and laugh. Thought it was a great joke on me.

Mickey never once let his great baseball fame affect him. He was always the same, a down-home country kid. We were both young kids. Mick was nineteen, I was twenty-one. Everyone thought because we were major-league players that we were mature adults. We were far from that. We were just kids and we acted like kids.

When we traveled from town to town with the Yankees, we went by train in those days, and we'd have our private car. We would have a couple of drinks and we'd start wrestling. He let me get my favorite hold on him, and I'd get as tight a grip as I could, and he'd break loose in a minute and throw me up against the wall like I was a toy. He was so strong. Then I'd come back and grab him again, he'd flex his muscles, and I'd go flying again.

One time I said, "I'm going to beat you on the train today." He said, "You're going to beat me?" I said, "Yes, today I'm going to beat you." We started wrestling. He said, "Get your favorite hold." I put my arms around him, and when he went to throw me, I got ahold of his lower front teeth with my fingers, and I held on for dear life. He couldn't eat for two days . . . .

We'd bring water guns into the clubhouse and we'd squirt water at each other and every player who came in. When the Polaroid cameras first came out, Joe Collins would be sitting on the toilet and we'd open the stall door and shoot pictures of him. . . .

George Weiss hated me from day one. When I came up in 1950, my first day with the club, we were losing, 9–0, in Boston and the Old Man (Casey) put me into the game. The first time up, I doubled off the left-field fence for one run, and later in the same inning, I got a single with the bases loaded for two more runs. Two hits in the same inning sparked the team and we came up from behind to win, 15–10, no kidding.

Casey liked me, I guess, because I was a lot like him, the way he was when he was a young player. I suppose I had a lot of balls for a rookie. But he was harder on me than anybody. I may have been his pet, but Casey still demanded more of me on the field.

Weiss wanted to send me down that first year. He was trying to get rid of George Stirnweiss, but couldn't make the deal; so until he did, he had to unload one other player to keep the roster at twenty-five, and he picked me. During all the fussing, I got to bat three times; the first time, I hit a three-run homer; another time I got a double, and the next time I walked. But he still insisted on sending me to Kansas City for thirty days till they got Stirnweiss straightened out.

Casey came to me and said he had to send me down for thirty days. Then he said: "But why ain't you mad? If it was me, I'd squawk to him." So I did. I went to his office and told Weiss that I thought it was a hell of

"George Weiss, the Yankees' general manager, hated me cause I spoke up to him, argued with him," said Billy Martin. "But Casey loved me. I guess because I was a lot like him as a kid, rough, tough, and scrappy. And I had a lot of balls."

a thing, that I didn't deserve to go back to the minors, and I ought to play with the Yankees. He really got pissed off at me for daring to argue with him. After that, even after he sent me down and I came back thirty days later, Weiss was on my tail. He even had detectives following me in spring training, and he said, "If I catch you stepping out of line, you're gone."

I began to room with Mickey and we were always together. He was more than a friend to me, he was more like my brother, even closer than brothers. I even spent an entire winter living with him and Merlyn back in Commerce in 1953. I don't know what kind of influence I was on him, but he wasn't a bad influence on me. He was a good influence.

One Sunday morning we were in the hotel in Boston and Mick ordered eggs for breakfast. They always had to be three-minute eggs, but this time they were only done one and a half minutes. So Mick left them on the table. In those days, it seemed that every time I threw something, I hit something. So I picked up the eggs and looked out the window and saw Vic Raschi and Rae Scarborough down on the street just getting into a cab to go to church and then the ballpark. I started to pitch the eggs out the window from the seventeenth floor. Mickey tried to stop me; and I still remember him yelling, "No, don't do it, Billy. Raschi is like a loon. He'll get crazy." But I let the eggs fly and you wouldn't believe it, the damned things dropped seventeen floors, hit the cabbie right between the eyes, and splattered all over Raschi and Scarborough. Damn! Then Mickey and I started piling all the furniture—chairs, tables, and every-thing—in front of the door like a blockade to keep them the hell out of the room because we knew they were heading up to our room to kick the living shit out of us.

Another time, when we went to Japan with the team, we went to a lot of places with our wives and they finally said one night that Mickey and Whitey Ford and I could go out on the town by ourselves, and they would just stay back at the hotel and rest up. So I was supposed to pick up the girls in Whitey's room, and I got there while he was in the bath-room, shaving. Whitey's wife, Joan, was in bed when I got there. But I said to her, "Move over." Then I got on the other side of the bed on top of the covers and all, and I was all dressed anyway. But I was lying there when Whitey was done shaving and came out of the bathroom, and I timed it just right. So I was saying to Joan, "When will Whitey get back, Joanie dear?" And when Whitey saw us, he broke up and fell on the floor, laughing.

That's how we three lived, like brothers, being part of each other's family.

12

WHITEY FORD TALKS ABOUT MANTLE

I began spending time with Mickey in 1953, my first year back from the Army. From what I knew, and it was little, I could never imagine having enough in common with Mickey to socialize with him. I figured we were incompatible. No two people could have been more different: me from the streets of New York, a wise, know-it-all city kid, him a hick from Oklahoma.

While I was in the Army, though, Mickey began hanging around with Billy Martin, so it was just natural for the three of us to get together when I returned to the Yankees. Most of the time we spent together was on road trips. When the team was in New York, I would go home to my family every night. Well, almost every night.

When I did see Mickey again, in 1953, he had changed. He had been in the major leagues for two years and had begun to take on a little sophistication. He was dressing nicely (no more jeans and cowboy boots), and he knew his way around town. I'm sure Billy had something to do with that.

And when I saw him play, I couldn't believe how good he was, how fast he ran, how much power he had in those big arms and neck.

Left: Whitey Ford and dog Snoopy in his study at his Lake Success home. "There's no question that Mickey Mantle was the greatest ballplayer I ever saw," said Whitey.

Below left: "While I was in the Army in 1950, Mickey began hanging around Billy Martin, and it was a most natural thing for the three of us to go around with each other when I was released," said Ford,

Below right: Whitey Ford, out of the Army after nearly two years, and Billy Martin enjoy a round of golf.

FORT MONMOUTH

HOME OF THE
SIGNAL CORPS
U.S. ARMY

I had first seen him play for a week or two back in 1950, when he came up from the minor leagues and traveled with us, and I heard and read a lot about his tremendous potential. But now that potential became a reality.

Back in 1950 he was a shortstop and a pretty bad one. He could hardly scoop up a ball, and when he did, he couldn't throw it straight. By 1953, the Yankees converted him to the outfield—he wasn't a good outfielder at first, but he became one. In those days, he would just outrun balls with his great speed, and he had a tremendous throwing arm.

I caught my first glimpse of his great batting power in Washington, when he hit a tremendous homer against Chuck Stobbs. The ball sailed clear out of the stadium and traveled about 600 feet. I think that was when I first became convinced that I was in the company of true greatness.

Looking back, there's no question that Mickey was the greatest ballplayer I ever saw. I'm not making comparisons between Mick and Joe DiMaggio because I can't. It wouldn't be fair. I played with DiMag just one season, 1950, and by that time he was at the end of his great career and was having a lot of physical problems. In fact, I saw Joe only a little more than half a season. When I joined the club in July, he was batting about .235 and he ended up hitting .301, so he must have hit .370 in the time I was there. He was still graceful and such a good hitter, it made me realize how great he must have been in his prime.

As far as Mickey is concerned, there are so many memories of great things he did on the field. But my greatest memories of him will always be the things we did off the field and the great fun we had together. He was the brother I never had.

After the 1955 season, the Yankees were invited to go to Japan on a goodwill tour. We were allowed to bring our wives, but Mickey's wife was pregnant and couldn't go. In the first couple of days of the trip, we met this four-hundred-pound sumo wrestler, and we thought it would be fun to go out on the town with him. Through an interpreter we invited him to join us. So we went out, the four of us—Mickey, Billy Martin, me, and this wrestler. We were buying him drinks and having a good time, and the wrestler hadn't said a word all night. All he did was smile whenever we said anything or whenever we gave him another drink.

After a few hours, we were getting loaded, and Billy couldn't resist having some fun. There we were with this huge wrestler who didn't know what we were saying. So when Billy winked and handed the wrestler a drink and said, "You open your mouth and I'll knock you on your ass," the wrestler smiled and just shook his head. Then I would say something insulting. Again, the wrestler would smile and shake his head.

Now it was 3:00 A.M. and time to call it a night. Billy spoke a little Japanese, so he said good night to the wrestler in Japanese. And the guy just looked at us and said clear as day, "Well, good night, fellows.

Thank you very much for a nice time." He spoke perfect English.

Billy, Mickey and I almost shit in our pants. The guy understood everything we had been saying and he was big enough to kill the three of us with his bare hands.

Good thing he had a great sense of humor.

Mickey hated being in Japan. He complained all the time he was there. He was homesick and he was tired from the long baseball season. He couldn't wait to get back to Commerce.

Then he got an idea. He had his business partner back home send him a cable to Japan: MERLYN EXPECTING BABY ANY MINUTE. PLEASE GET HOME IMMEDIATELY.

Mickey showed the cable to Stengel, and Casey showed it to Commissioner Ford Frick, and Mickey took the first plane out to the States. The baby was born in January. We each got a check for $3,500 to make the trip. When Mickey got his check, most of the money had been taken away in the form of a fine.

We played three games in Manila after coming back from Japan, and the one thing that made an impression on me was a school building back of the ballpark. Painted on the school walls were signs that read: BABE RUTH HIT ONE HERE; LEFTY O'DOUL HIT ONE HERE; LOU GEHRIG HIT A HOME RUN HERE.

There was a fellow in Commerce named Roy Crow. He was slightly retarded, but he was a harmless guy who was loved by the entire town. Everybody tried to make him feel important. The bank gave him a bank-book and a checking account, and he'd get up every morning and make a deposit of five cents in the account, then he'd go to the store to buy an ice cream cone and he'd write a check to pay for it.

He idolized Mantle. His whole life was coming to Mickey's house, wearing his Yankee cap, and sitting on the stoop and talking to Mickey. He had a crush on Mickey's sister, Barbara, and Mickey used to tease him about it.

One day, when we were there, Roy Crow showed up. I was in the kitchen with Mickey, and Billy was still asleep in the bedroom. Mickey began to tease the boy.

Roy called Billy "Bill Barton," and Mickey said to him, "You know, Roy, I think Barbara likes Bill Barton. I think he kissed her last night."

All of a sudden Roy went storming through the house. He ran into the bedroom where Billy was fast asleep, jumped on the bed, and began pounding Billy on the chest. Billy didn't know what the hell was going on except he'd been awakened in a strange house and there was some guy pounding on his chest. When he finally awakened and realized what was happening, he joined us in the kitchen. We were laughing so hard, we couldn't eat.

It was in the middle of the 1957 season that our "unholy trio" came to a sad end.

It was a Sunday, and Mickey and I had planned a big birthday party for Billy that night after the game. Monday was a day off, so we could all stay out late Sunday night. We invited most of the team to come to the party at the Copa, one of New York's great nightclubs. There was Yogi Berra, Gil McDougald, Johnny Kucks, Hank Bauer, Moose Skowron, and me, plus all the wives. Mickey and Billy came stag.

After a dinner at Danny's Hideaway, we went to the Copa to catch Sammy Davis, Jr.'s, last show. There was another group not too far from us, sitting at the bar, which was near a long table. It turned out that it was a bowling team and they had been there for several hours. That was obvious because they were pretty well juiced and they were making a lot of noise. They started calling Sammy Davis "Sambo" and making other racial remarks like that.

Suddenly Hank Bauer, ex-Marine hero and one of the toughest guys in or out of baseball, yelled for the noisy crowd to shut up. Next thing one of their guys said, "Who's going to make me?" Then this guy got up and it looked like he and Bauer were going to go at each other. They walked into a back room, and the rest of us got up to follow just in case there was real trouble.

The guy who made the crack at Bauer got to the back before any of us. All of a sudden, we heard a crash, and by the time we got there, the big guy was stretched out flat on the floor. My eyes never left Hank, so I know he didn't hit the guy. To this day, I don't know who slugged the guy. I think it might have been one of the Copa bouncers, because it was a real professional job.

I knew one thing: We had to get out of there, and fast. If this hit the papers, all of us would be in deep trouble. One of the bouncers led us out through the back door into the lobby and out to our cars and then home.

Next morning I got a call from Mickey and Billy, telling me that George Weiss wanted to see us at his office at eleven. We were going to be fined $1,000 each. It was already ten.

"I'm not coming. I can't get there by eleven. Let me know what happened."

Mickey and Billy went to Weiss's office, and in addition to the fines they imposed on us, we had to tell our story to a grand jury. The guy who had been hit complained to the district attorney, and we were in up to our ears.

Finally, after telling our story to the grand jury, we met with the guy and his lawyer and we settled out of court. The guy got a $6,500 settlement. So, between the fine and the lawyer's fee, it cost each of us $2,000 for doing nothing.

We all think that George Weiss made Billy the scapegoat because he never really liked him and he was looking for an excuse to get rid of him. Funny thing is that the whole thing had nothing to do with Billy. He didn't organize the party; Mickey and I did. It just happened that it was Billy's birthday.

Exactly a month to the day after the Copa incident, Billy was traded to Kansas City. It was no coincidence.

13

MANTLE
TALKS ABOUT
HIS BEST PAL

My best pal on the Yankees during my early years with the club was Billy Martin. Billy joined the Yankees in 1950, the year before I came up to stay, and except for 1954 and part of 1955, when he was in the Army, we were close as brothers. That is, until June 1957, when general manager George Weiss traded Billy to Kansas City. Billy had been a very good player for the Yankees. In particular, he was outstanding in a close pennant race or a World Series. He just seemed to come up with the big plays when we needed them.

But when he was traded and left us, it seemed something went out of him. The great fighting spirit, the zest, something. Maybe because after he left the Yankees he was always moving from team to team. From KC to Detroit. Then to Cleveland in 1958. Cincinnati got him, then Milwaukee, and then to Minnesota in 1961. It's pretty tough to play your best when you're with seven different clubs in a five-year span.

But with the Yankees from 1950 to 1957, Martin was a valuable member of some great teams—a spirited, clutch batter who lifted team spirits in every game he was in.

He was certainly a hothead, I'll admit that. In his major-league career he had a lot of fights with catcher Clint Courtney, Jimmy Piersall, and others, with managers, club officials, and, of course, with umpires all over the league.

When Billy became manager he fought his players tooth and nail trying to get them to hustle every day and to win. He battled with club owners to get more money for his players and, on occasion, he even fought with sportscasters and broadcasters who were announcing the games.

It may have been that Billy's upbringing had to do with all that. He had a very rough childhood. From the time he was a little kid, he had to fight. He was skinny kid with a big nose, and kids called him "Pinocchio" and "banana nose," and then he fought them. He came from a very poor home in Berkeley; his father deserted Billy as a small boy, and Billy never knew him until he was an adult, and the family never had any money. Billy would have to sweep up and work around a church nearby to earn food money for the family. Matter of fact, Billy moved out of his mother's house and moved next door to his aunt and then a grandmother because his mother could not support her small family.

Billy grew up interested in baseball and not much else. He was a fighter and scrapper and all through the sandlot days and high school ball, Billy was fighting and clawing his way to some kind of local recognition.

One day Billy got into a rough fight in a high school game and got thrown off the team. I saw a picture that a local photographer took of Billy in street clothes watching the team practice. It was one of the saddest pictures I ever saw.

When he broke into professional baseball, he had an even tougher time because he was so scrawny-looking. Billy is bigger than he looks—and has real strong arms and legs—but he isn't very big as baseball players go. More than that, he has a very boyish face that made him look younger and smaller. The baseball scouts ignored Billy most of the time—they were looking for the bigger, power-hitting guys. So he had to scramble and push and fight to get some attention. He had to act twice as cocky just to get to the point where he could begin to show people how well he could play ball.

And the thing was, he didn't have a lot of natural ability. He had to use brains and hustle and sharp observations to make his skills valuable to a team. He'd argue with managers because he wanted them to pay attention to him so that he could show them what he could do. And managers like Casey Stengel and Charlie Dressen, both of whom managed him, appreciated that attitude. He'd fight anybody who started a fight with one of his teammates, and he'd argue with an umpire because he wanted to win. I never knew anybody who hated to lose as badly as Billy did.

I clearly remember the 1955 World Series, when Johnny Podres shut out the Yankees in the final game to give the Brooklyn Dodgers their first World Series championship ever, and Casey Stengel his first World Series defeat as Yankee manager. A long time after the game was over, when Yankee Stadium was practically empty, Billy was still in his uniform in the clubhouse. He had tears in his eyes. He said, "We should have won. It isn't right for a man like Casey to lose. It's a shame for a man like that to lose."

This feeling of having to win used to wear Billy out. I think it's one of those things that ended his playing career so quickly after he left the Yankees. He needed to win—had to win—but the ballclubs he went to finished seventh and fifth and like that. I think he couldn't take the idea of losing, and that it ruined him as a player. He was only thirty-three when he was released by Minnesota.

I can remember when Billy drove himself so hard that he was playing on pure nerve. That was in 1953. he couldn't sleep. He fidgeted all the time, he couldn't eat. At one point over a period of about four weeks, he lost almost 30 pounds—and he weighed only about 175 pounds to begin with. He was pretty nearly a physical wreck. Yet that year he played in 149 games of our 154-game schedule, went to bat 587 times, scored 72 runs, and batted in 75. He did it all on guts, on pure hang-on courage. His batting average was only .257 that season, and when you think of his runs-batted-in total and the fact that he wasn't a power hitter, you know that just about every hit he got must have come in a clutch situation.

But "clutch" was the key to Billy. Because he was loud and cocky and aggressive, people thought he was all mouth and argument. They forgot the courage he had. The tougher things got, the better Billy played. He had the sort of spirit that reacted to a situation. Some people freeze or feel sick when they find themselves in a difficult spot. Not Billy. He came through. The figures proved it.

In the World Series, where you really feel the pressure, where everything is clutch play, Billy had a lifetime average of .333, or 76 points higher than his career season average. That's for five World Series. I looked up in the record book to see how Billy's Series record compared to Babe Ruth's. The Babe was one of the greatest World Series performers ever; look it up sometime and you'll be amazed at the things he did. But the Babe, with 129 Series at-bats, hit 7 points less than Billy—.326 to .333.

Billy's greatest Series was in 1953, the year he almost fell apart from nervous exhaustion. We beat the Dodgers in six games that year, and that was a really fine Dodger team. They couldn't stop Billy. He went three for four in the first game, including a triple, batted in three runs, and stole a base. He went two for three in the second and hit a home run. In the third game he went one for three and scored one of our two runs. In the fourth game he went two for four, including a triple and batted two runs. In the fifth game he went two for five, hit his second home run, and drove in two runs. In the sixth and last game, he went two for five and batted in two runs.

He had 12 hits in the six games, the most anyone has ever had in a six-game Series, and no one, not even in a seven-game Series, has ever had more than 12. It was really fitting that Billy Martin won the Babe Ruth Trophy for being the World Series' outstanding player.

Billy has gone on to become one of the leading managers in baseball. First with the Minnesota Twins, the Detroit Tigers, the Texas Rangers, and then the "dream job" of his entire life—manager of the great New York Yankees.

To my mind, this is the essence of what America is all about—a poor, scrawny little kid, with little background, education, yet able to go on to become one of the great success stories in sports.

14

TRIPLE CROWN
WINNER

Allie Reynolds quit baseball after the 1954 season, and now of the Big Three whose pitching had played so great a part in the Yankees' success after Stengel—Reynolds, Raschi, and Lopat—only Lopat was left.

In December 1954, George Weiss made a mammoth trade with the Baltimore Orioles, and among the players exchanged were two pitchers

Right: A trade brought two top pitchers to the Yankees in late 1954. In photo: (L) Bob Turley and (R) Don Larsen. Both players were acquired from the Orioles in a five-man deal. Center is Whitey Ford.

Opposite page: Casey Stengel had been after Mantle to cut down on his strikeouts. Mickey began to wait for the better pitches. He changed his stance, crowded the plate more than he had, and it began to pay off. In the first month of the 1955 season, Mickey slammed out a record 10 home runs, most of them gigantic drives that brought acclaim from the fans.

he wanted badly—Don Larsen and Bob Turley. Both pitchers were to pay off with remarkable records.

Mickey Mantle was coming off a season when he slugged 27 homers and hit for a .300 batting average in 1954. He was still a kid, just twenty-three years old, earning more than $20,000 a year, and his best years were ahead if he didn't injure himself.

In 1955, Mickey changed his batting stance at the start of the season, crowding the plate more, trying to cut down on his strikeouts, and it began to pay off. In the first month of the season, Mantle drove out 10 home runs, most of them gigantic drives that had the fans shouting their approval.

On May 13, against the Detroit Tigers, Mickey faced a tough right-handed pitcher, Steve Gromek. Andy Carey was on first base with one out. The count went to two and two, and Mickey set himself for the next pitch. In came Gromek's fastball, right across the belt line, and Mickey sent the pitch crashing some 400 feet into the bleachers. The Yanks now had a 2–0 lead.

In the third inning, with Hank Bauer on base, Mickey drove a scorching drive to center that scored Hank.

In the fifth inning, Mickey batting left-handed again, faced Gromek with a two-ball, no-strike count, and crashed a line drive that traveled some 450 feet into the bleachers for a second home run.

In the eighth inning, against Bob Miller, Mickey, batting right-handed, slugged Miller's first pitch into the center-field bleachers, his third home run of the day. The Yanks won the game, 5–2, and all five runs were driven in by Mantle. It was the first time in American League history that the same player had hit home runs in a game batting left-handed and right-handed.

Later in the season Mickey again slugged three home runs in a game against Baltimore, batting left-handed and right-handed.

On May 16 Mickey was hitting a solid .311 and had just finished a remarkable weekend. He hit four for four against the Tigers, two hits in four at-bats the next day, and four hits in nine in a doubleheader at Yankee Stadium against Kansas City. Mantle's hitting streak was now the talk of the league, and the rest of the team, inspired by his tremendous batting average, played brilliant baseball the rest of the way.

In the All-Star game, Mickey smashed a three-run home run, but the National League team won the game in twelve innings.

Sparked by Mantle's slugging and the inspiration provided by Billy Martin's return from the Army, the Yankees went on a tear, drove into first place over the Indians, and took their seventh pennant in nine years by three games over

Billy Martin had the ability to spark a team, and when he returned to the Yankees late in 1955, they drove into first place over Cleveland. Greeting Martin on his first day back, Yogi Berra is all smiles.

Cleveland. The Indians' management, which had already sold more than $3 million worth of Series tickets, mailed back refunds with the words "We're Sorry" on the envelope.

Playing in 147 games, despite several injuries, Mickey batted .306, slugged 37 home runs, hit 11 triples, and drove in 99 runs. It was a banner year for "the Mick," but because of a serious thigh injury, he was not in condition to play his best in the World Series against the Brooklyn Dodgers.

In the first game, the Yankees slam-banged Dodger ace Don Newcombe for three home runs in the first six innings, two by Joe Collins, and beat the Brooks, 6–5.

Then Tommy Byrne held the Dodgers to just five hits, and the Yankees took game number two, 4–2, by scoring all of their runs in the fourth inning.

"We gotta win this one," Dodger star Jackie Robinson told his teammates before the third game. "If we lose again, they'll be calling us choke-up guys for the rest of our lives. Do we want that?"

In the third game, the Dodgers started Carl Erskia who had been knocked out in the first game, but this time the Dodgers got him two runs in the first, second, fourth, and seventh innings, he went the distance, and they took game three. Then, in game four, home runs by Campanella, Duke Snider, and Gil Hodges gave the Dodgers an 8–5 victory, and the Series was now tied at two games.

Now Dodger manager Walt Alston came back with a rookie pitcher, Roger Craig, for the fifth game, and the Dodger hitters made it work. Duke Snider slugged out two home runs and Sandy Amoros another, and the Yankees had been pushed near to the brink of disaster as the Dodgers won the game, 5–3.

And all of Brooklyn went nuts at this turn of events.

Now Alston again gambled, with twenty-four-year-old Karl Spooner, who had sparkled during the Dodgers' past several regular-season games. But Spooner lasted just one-third of an inning as the Yankees pounded him for five runs, including a three-run blast by Bill Skowron, and the Yankees cruised by 5–1. The Yankee victory forced a seventh game, one that is still talked about in Brooklyn.

In this vital game, the Yankees faced Johnny Podres and the twenty-three-year old celebrating his birthday on that date, pitched magnificently as the Dodgers provided him with a 2–0 lead into the sixth inning.

Then the Yankees started their move. Billy Martin singled and Gil McDougald walked. There were no

Beset by injuries to his ankle and thigh, Mickey slugged out 37 home runs and ended the season with a batting average of .306. Photo shows Mantle on crutches leaving hotel room before the end of the 1955 season.

In the first game of the 1955 World Series, the Yanks' first baseman, Joe Collins, belted two home runs off Dodger pitcher Don Newcombe to win 6-5.

A daring attempted steal of home backfires as Dodger catcher Roy Campanella blocks the plate and tags out Billy Martin in the sixth inning of the 1955 World Series opener at Yankee Stadium on September 28. Umpire Bill Summers calls Martin out as pinch-hitter Eddie Robinson of Yanks watches. The Yanks won, 6-5.

In the eighth inning of the first game of the World Series, Jackie Robinson (42) astounded the Yankees and the crowd with a clean steal of home. Robinson starts his slide as Yogi Berra awaits the pitch from Whitey Ford. Umpire Bill Summers called Robinson safe as the crowd roared for a full five minutes.

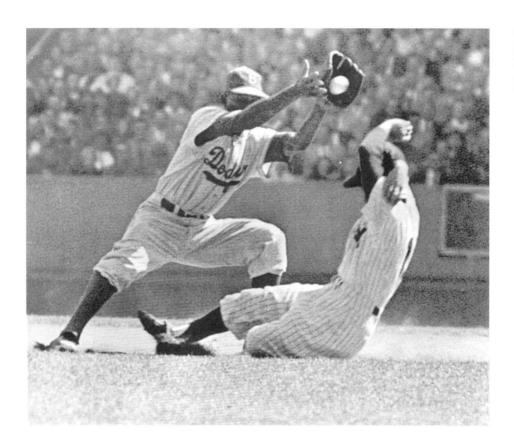

October 3, 1955. Yankee shortstop Phil Rizzuto and Dodger second baseman Junior Gilliam on Phil's successful steal in the second inning at Yankee Stadium.

Top: Johnny Podres kicks, fires, and follows through with a pitch in third game of the World Series against the Yankees at Ebbets Field. Podres celebrated his twenty-third birthday with an 8-3 Dodger win over the Yanks. The Yankees held a 2-1 edge in the Series at that point.

Middle: Yankee catcher Yogi Berra rips into umpire Bill Summers with a verbal barrage in eighth inning of 1955 World Series opener at Yankee Stadium after the umpire rules Jackie Robinson safe on steal of home.

Bottom: Roy Campanella learned what happens when you get hit by a former Purdue football star, Bill Skowron. Campanella attempts to block the plate as Skowron scores. Campanella was charged with an error.

Above: A marvelous action shot in
the fifth inning of the fourth game of
the Series. Pee Wee Reese is shown
after beating out an infield single
and is called safe by ump Bill
Summers. Yankee pitcher Johnny
Kucks (53) was too late tagging
Reese (1). Joe Collins, Yankee first
baseman, is at left.

Right: Yankee first baseman Bill
Skowron is congratulated by Mickey
Mantle after his three-run home run
beat the Dodgers in the sixth game
of the 1955 World Series by a 5-1
score. The Yankee win forced a
seventh and deciding game.

Even as early as 1951, Mantle, like Joe DiMaggio, the legend he was to replace, looked great in the famous pinstripe uniform. Under the instruction of Tommy Henrich, Mantle proved to be a very capable outfielder. (Photofile/PF Sports Images)

OPPOSITE PAGE: "I've been arguing with Mantle for two years to be more patient at the plate and only swing at the good ones," said Casey Stengel. Finally in 1956 it paid off, and Mantle became the MVP. (Photofile/PF Sports Images)

LEFT: One of the Yankees' brightest prospects in 1957, Tony Kubek (left) is shown with Mickey Mantle and Gil McDougald.

BELOW: These Yankee stars are prepared and waiting for the Pittsburgh Pirates in the opening game of the 1960 World Series. (L-R) Roger Maris, Yogi Berra, Mickey Mantle, Ellie Howard, Moose Skowron and Johnny Blanchard. In the first game Maris hit a home run but the Pirates won 6-2. In game No. 2, Mantle hit two of the longest home runs ever seen and the Yanks won 16 to 3.

LEFT: In a four game Series against the White Sox, Maris slugged out four homers to give him a total of 40. Now he was 24 games ahead of Babe Ruth's record of 60 in a single season. Mantle was right on Roger's heels with 38 homers. Mickey, too, was ahead of Ruth's record and fans all over the country were getting excited.

BELOW: New York Yankee Teammates Mickey Mantle, Roger Maris and Dick Stuart before the start of a World Series game against the Pittsburgh Pirates in 1960.

OPPOSITE PAGE: Following the 1963 World Series, Ralph Houk was named General Manager of the Yankees. In turn Houk appointed Yogi Berra the new Yankee Manager for 1964. Berra met with Mickey Mantle to inquire about Mickey's physical condition and Mickey congratulated Yogi and wished him the very best. At Yankee Stadium, Berra and Mantle talk things over.

OPPOSITE PAGE: Another towering Yankee Stadium blast, this time against the Washington Senators in the mid 1960s, when a homerun had to carry all the way into the seats, not just over the modern day fence. (Photofile/PF Sports Images)

LEFT: Closeup of a Yankee immortal.

BELOW: Mantle at the start of his fifteenth season with the Yankees, looking forward to a great season in 1966.

LEFT: Baseball Commissioner Bowie Kuhn is shown congratulating Mickey Mantle as Mantle was voted into Baseball's Hall of Fame in 1974.

BELOW RIGHT: Mantle reflects during an interview at his New York City restaurant in July. Behind Mantle is a montage of New York Yankee photos. Mantle says of the 1961 Yankees, "That was the best team I ever saw and the best team I ever played on."

BELOW CENTER: Mickey Mantle gets a hug and kiss from Reggie Jackson during the Yankees' 45th Old-Timers Classic Ceremony at Yankee Stadium July 27, 1991 as Ron Guidry (right) and Whitey Ford watch and applaud.

Above: The 1955 World Champions: Pee Wee Reese, Carl Furillo, Ray Campanella, Duke Snider, Gil Hodges, Junior Gilliam, Jackie Robinson, Don Zimmer, Johnny Podres, Clem Labine, Don Newcombe, Don Hoak, Frank Kellert, Meyer, George Shuba, Carl Erskine, Billy Loes, Bessent, Roger Craig, Karl Spooner, Ed Roebuck, manager Walt Alston, secretary Lee Scott, Charley Digiovanna (batboy).

Left: Duke Snider, Pee Wee Reese, and Mickey Mantle, 1955 World Series.

outs, and Yankee slugger Yogi Berra came up to hit. Yogi hit a sharp drive out to left field, and it seemed as if the ball would go into the lower portion of the left-field stands. Then Amoros, running at full speed, cut over, racing toward the ball, and with his right arm fully extended, gloved the ball for a miraculous catch, then pivoted and heaved the ball to second to double McDougald. It was a play that provided Brooklyn fans with chills and thrills for years to come. The Yankees threatened in the eighth, but Podres's gritty pitching cut them down, and the Dodgers had won the Series.

President Eisenhower recovered fully from his fall heart attack, and in the early spring of 1956 the powerful Republican incumbent ignored the upcoming presidential election, leaving Democrats Estes Kefauver and Adlai Stevenson to battle each other for their party's nomination while he kept an eye on the dangerous Middle East situation. Inside the United States, a revolution was fomenting as a result of a U.S. Supreme Court ruling that held public school segregation to be unconstitutional.

"Before 1956 I was doing pretty well," said Mickey Mantle, "but I wasn't Joe DiMaggio. But in 1956 I hit the jackpot, by winning the Triple Crown and leading the American League and the majors with a .353 batting average, and hitting 52 home runs. My biggest kick was in beating out my idol, Ted Williams, for the batting title."

But the problems of the world did not concern Casey Stengel or Mickey Mantle of the Yankees in their pursuit of another pennant and World Series title.

"Before 1956, I was doing pretty well," said Mantle, "but I wasn't Babe Ruth or Joe DiMaggio. But in 1956 I started to do the things that every expert thought I should do.

"I won the Triple Crown, leading the American League and the majors in batting average with a .353 average; I hit 52 home runs (my best year yet) and had 130 runs batted in. The only previous players to lead both leagues in these categories were Rogers Hornsby in 1925, Lou Gehrig in 1934, and Ted Williams in 1942. In addition, my total bases of 376, 132 runs scored, and a .705 slugging average gave me the American League's MVP (Most Valuable Player) Award.

"Now, all these honors were terrific, but my biggest kick was in beating out Ted Williams for the batting title. It was a horse race down to the final few days of the season, with both of us hitting .348. Then I went into Boston, got six hits, and passed him. Somebody asked Ted what he thought about it. He said, 'If I could run like that son of a bitch, I'd hit .400 every year.'"

Casey Stengel had his headaches in spring training in 1956. Early in camp, Mantle once again pulled his hamstring muscle and was unable to run for a few days. Gil McDougald, the shortstop, hurt his knees when he fell on a wet pavement in Miami. Bob Cerv pulled a stomach muscle, Ellie Howard fractured a couple of fingers, and Norm Siebern, a classy

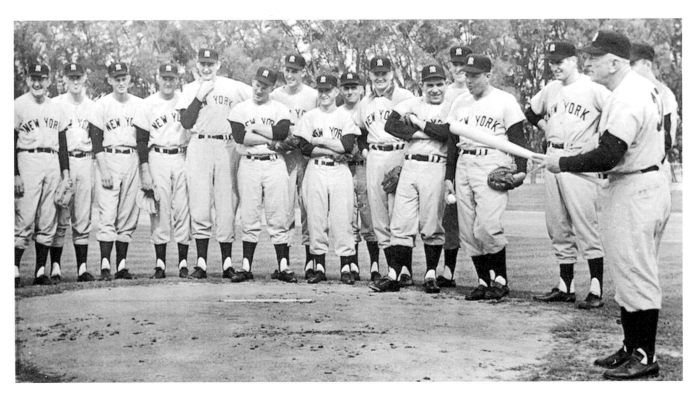

Casey Stengel, using his bat to illustrate a point, opened spring training at St. Petersburg, February 21, 1956.

In spring training 1956, the Yankees had so many injuries that the dressing room looked like a hospital. Mickey Mantle injured his thigh again; Ellie Howard fractured a couple of fingers; Bob Cerv pulled a stomach muscle; and shortstop Gil McDougald in the photo hurt his knees. But by the time the season opened on April 5, most of the injuries had healed, and the team was headed for another pennant race.

outfielder, crashed into a concrete wall chasing a fly ball and jammed his kneecap. Billy Hunter and Irv Noren had suffered injuries. All in all, the Yankees' spring training period looked as busy as the emergency room of a small hospital.

A number of new faces were in camp this year: Norm Siebern, who had been an outfield star in Birmingham; Tony Kubek, a tall infielder, who hit for a .334 average at Quincy in the Three-I League; Bobby Richardson, a twenty-one-year-old infielder, who hit .296 at Denver; Jerry Lumpe, who hit .301 at Birmingham; and Luis Aparicio all looked as if they were ready for the Yankees.

And Casey's pet protégé, Mickey Mantle, never worked harder in his life than he worked in 1956. He cut down his strikeouts by being more patient at the plate. He struck out only once in the entire spring training period. He also adjusted his stance to make him less vulnerable to tight pitches across the letters—pitches that caused him the most trouble.

"Those pitchers have thrown me plenty of balls

There were a number of bright prospects at St. Petersburg in 1956, including Tony Kubek, who hit .334 for Quincy in the Three-I League; Bobby Richardson, who hit .296 at Denver; Clete Boyer; and Joe Pepitone. And they all looked as if they would make the team. (L-R) Clete Boyer, Tony Kubek, Bobby Richardson, and Joe Pepitone.

In 1956 Mickey Mantle worked in spring training to cut down on his strikeouts. He listened to Casey Stengel, who had been advising him to be more patient at the plate. And when the season opened, Mickey began to hit the longest home runs seen in recent years.

from the belt up and inside with plenty of stuff on them, and I couldn't do much about them. Now I'm hitting them much better," said Mantle.

Mantle seemed to be hitting all types of pitches better in spring training. In one game against the Cards, Mantle lined a ball toward right center field. Stan Musial, playing right field, turned and watched the ball sail high over the fence. Afterward Stan said, "No home run ever cleared my head by so much height before. Mick looks different this year. He always struck out a lot, but now he's letting bad pitches go. If he hits 60 homers and bats .400, I can't say I'd be surprised."

A few days later, against the Dodgers in Miami, Mickey drove two successive pitches over the center-field fence for home runs. The next day, in St. Petersburg, Mickey clouted the ball to deep center field for another homer. On the trip homeward, Mantle drove out long home runs in Jacksonville, Savannah, and Atlanta.

"I think," said Hank Bauer, "that our country cousin from Commerce is gonna be quite a player this year. He's older, more experienced, and now, for the first time in five years, he's serious about filling Joe DiMaggio's shoes."

President Ike Eisenhower opened the 1956 season for the Washington Senators by tossing the first ball. But Mantle quickly grabbed the spotlight by driving pitcher Camilo Pascual's first pitch over the center-field fence for one of the longest drives ever seen in the Senators' ballpark. In the sixth inning of the game, with two men on base, Mickey slammed another drive over the center-field fence. This was the first time that any player ever hit two home runs in one game over the center-field

barrier at Griffith Stadium. The standing-room-only crowd of some 32,000 fans, led by President Eisenhower, joined in a tremendous roar of applause for the Yankee slugger.

After the game ended, Mickey was escorted to the president's private box, and as he approached him, the president thrust his hand out and shook Mickey's hand.

"Mickey, that was powerful slugging you did out there this afternoon. I don't think I've ever seen anyone ever hit a ball farther. You know, I do know something about the game. I played some ball at West Point."

Mickey was awed and embarrassed. "Thank you, Mr. President. Thank you very much."

Back in the dugout, Mickey said, "Can you imagine the president of the United States shaking my hand? And me a former miner from

Commerce. I sure wish Dad could have seen that today. Maybe," said Mickey, "I guess he did after all."

Three days later, the Yankees opened their home season against the Red Sox at the Stadium, and Whitey Ford held the slugging Bosox to just five hits as Mantle blasted out a towering home run and single and drove in four runs as the Yankees took a 7–1 victory. Three days later, against the Kansas City A's, Mickey staged a one-man batting exhibition, smashing out two home runs and then dropping a bunt down the third-base line to score another run in a 5–2 win.

Two days later, against Cleveland, Mickey's home run in the seventh inning chalked up another Yankee win.

The barrage continued. Mickey slugged 16 home runs in May, giving him twenty in the Yankees first 41 games.

On May 5, Mickey hit two home runs against Kansas City, then two more against Cleveland on May 18. On May 30, he turned in a rare feat.

It was the bottom of the fifth inning in a game at Yankee Stadium against the Senators. The Yankees had two men on base, and Mickey came up to hit against Pedro Ramos.

Ramos held the runners on base, then whipped in a fast ball, waist high, as Mickey got set for the pitch. He crouched slightly, then tore into the ball. Every ounce of muscle in his great body, shoulders, forearms, and wrists went into the drive, and the ball streaked higher and higher toward the very top of the Stadium. No one, not Babe Ruth, Lou Gehrig nor Joe DiMaggio had ever hit a ball over the third tier and out of the

Opposite page: In 1956 Mantle slugged out 16 home runs in the month of May to give him 20 homers in the Yankees' first 41 games.

Left: In this photo, the dotted lines in this air view of Yankee Stadium show the route of Mickey Mantle's gigantic home run against the Senators on May 30, 1956. The ball Mickey hit traveled some 465 feet and landed under the scoreboard in right-center field. It was one of the longest drives ever seen at the Stadium.

Stadium. The ball Mantle hit struck about two feet short of the top of the facade of the last tier for one of the longest home runs ever hit at the Stadium.

Afterward there was head-shaking by veteran players and current stars. Bill Dickey, an all-time Yankee great, said, "I've seen lots of hitters come and go, but Mickey has more power than any player I've ever seen. He's unbelievable."

The great Giant star Mel Ott said, "I think this kid Mantle is the most amazing player in the game today. I have never seen such speed, strength, and coordination. He's much improved over last year. You can't fool him that much anymore. And he's going to get even better as he goes along."

By early June, Mickey led the league in runs batted in with 52 runs scored with 47, 21 home runs, and 70 hits. His batting average at this stage of the season was .407.

Now, for the first time in his career, Mickey was living up to all of the expectations. Single-handedly he sparked the Yankees to victory after victory, clubbing out the longest home runs plus extra-base hits to pile up a lead over the other teams in the American League.

On May 16 the Yankees defeated Cleveland, and for the rest of the season, with Mantle and catcher Yogi Berra supplying most of the fire-power, kept the Yanks either in first place, or on the heels of the Indians, who were at the top of the league.

After the July 10 All-Star break, the Yanks swept three games from the Indians when Hank Bauer slugged a grand slam to win game one. In the second game, pitcher Tom Sturdevant hurled a two-hitter. And in the third game after Mickey hit his thirtieth home run, Billy Martin singled with the bases loaded to beat Bob Feller.

At the same time, the White Sox lost three straight games, and the Yanks vaulted into first place, never to relinquish it that season in the American League.

Now it was August 25, Old Timers' Day at the Stadium, and the old stars were cavorting about the field while some of the Yankees took their pictures.

Phil Rizzuto, their thirty-eight-year-old All-Star shortstop, was one of those shooting pictures. Phil didn't realize how soon it would be before he would become one of the old-timers.

This day, George Weiss and Stengel called Rizzuto into Casey's office and Weiss said, "We're going over the roster, Phil. Siebern and

Old-Timers' Day at Yankee Stadium in 1956. On Old Timers' Day, dozens of former Yankee stars appear and play several innings to please the fans who always throng to this affair. Appearing in this photo (L-R): Yogi Berra, Mickey Mantle, Joe DiMaggio and coach Ralph Houk.

In photo (L-R): Joe Collins, Billy Martin, Phil Rizzuto, and Gil McDougald

Noren are hurt, and we need another left-handed-hitting outfielder for the World Series. We want to go over this list with you to determine the logical player we can let go."

Rizzuto, flattered that Stengel and Weiss thought so highly of his opinion, agreed. Phil went down the list and named one player after another. But they were all rejected by Weiss. Finally, after going over the list several times, it dawned on Phil. Finally Weiss summoned the nerve to tell Phil what he had in mind. It was Rizzuto who was going to be released. Stengel had McDougald, Coleman, and Billy Martin to play shortstop, and Phil was clearly over the hill. Rizzuto's major-league career, which began in 1941, was over—in a flash.

In tears, Rizzuto quickly emptied his locker and left the clubhouse and drove home before the other players learned he was cut. Ex-Yankee George Stirnweiss, who had experienced the same rejection a few years earlier, accompanied Rizzuto. George was afraid Phil was going to jump off the George Washington Bridge, he was so crushed. Rizzuto, though bitter, wisely did not criticize the Yankee management. The following year he was hired as the team's broadcaster, joining Mel Allen and Red Barber.

In time Allen and Barber were fired, while Rizzuto remained at the Yankee microphones until 1995.

In September, when Mickey needed 14 home runs to beat Babe Ruth's mark, he slowed down. He was only able to hit five the entire month. But by this time, he was more concerned about reaching another goal. He wanted very much to be the American League's first Triple Crown winner since 1947.

On September 1, Mickey was paid an enormous compliment. The President of the United States came to see him play against the Senators. This was not an official visit, such as the one all presidents make when they throw out the opening ball. Ike Eisenhower, a great baseball fan, appeared in a surprise visit at the ball park. He informed his press secretary, Jim Haggerty, that he just wanted to watch Mantle add to his home-run string.

There was, however, one problem facing the President: Which team would he root for? Most fans knew that Ike was a great fan of the Senators. But he was coming chiefly to see Mantle hit a home run.

Ike solved the problem quite simply when he shook Mantle's hand while the cameras clicked. "I'll hit a homer for you, Mr. President," said Mickey.

"I do hope you hit a home run, Mickey, but I hope the Senators beat the Yankees."

Mickey came through as he promised the president. He smashed number forty-seven in the game as the Yanks went on to win.

On September 18, the Yankees played a night game against the White Sox at Comiskey Park. A win would clinch the American League pennant for the Yankees. The game went into the eleventh inning as Mantle came up to hit against gutsy Billy Pierce.

Pierce tried to fool Mickey with a curve that dropped off the table, but the Mick, going down with the pitch, slammed the ball out of the park in a tremendous blast for home run number fifty. Mickey's drive won the game and the pennant.

On September 28, just two days before the end of the season, Mickey led Ted Williams for the batting title, Al Kaline for the RBI crown, and everyone for the home-run title. That day, Mantle went one for four; the one hit was his 52nd homer, and it gave him a .353 batting average to Williams' .348. It gave Mickey 128 runs batted in to 124 for Kaline.

On September 30, the last day of the season, Mickey drove in his 130th run and won the batting title. But Kaline had 128 RBIs and was still playing a game with the Tigers.

Mickey was too nervous to hang around the Stadium for the final results. He went to the apartment he shared with Billy Martin, and there he heard that Kaline had been unable to overtake Mickey.

It was official: MICKEY WAS THE TRIPLE CROWN CHAMPION.

This was Mantle's greatest year as he led the league in batting with a .353 average, in home runs with 52, and in runs batted in with 130. His name went into the record book in distinguished company. Only six others had accomplished that feat in the major leagues. Rogers Hornsby, Jimmie Foxx, Chuck Klein, Lou Gehrig, Joe Medwick, and Ted Williams.

Mickey Mantle had fulfilled every expectation made of him when he

In 1956 Mickey Mantle won the Triple Crown to join such immortals as Rogers Hornsby, Lou Gehrig, Joe Medwick, Ted Williams, and Jimmy Foxx. Now Mantle was considered by many the greatest player in baseball.

first joined the Yankees as a scared, shy kid of nineteen in 1951. *Now he was the greatest player in baseball.*

Once more, the Yankees faced the Dodgers in the World Series. However, there would be no repetition of the outcome of the year before, although the Dodgers won the first two games, played at Ebbets Field.

In the first game Sal Maglie held the Yankees to nine scattered hits, including home runs by Mantle and Billy Martin, but Gil Hodges and Jackie Robinson homered off Whitey Ford, who was knocked out in three innings. In the second game Don Larsen started against Don Newcombe. Both pitchers were routed in the first inning, but the Dodgers, coming from six runs behind, won a slugfest by 13–8.

Back at Yankee Stadium, the Yankees picked up two games to even the Series. Whitey Ford, making his second start, held the Dodgers to eight hits as Enos Slaughter's homer with two men on base in the sixth inning and Billy Martin's round-tripper in the ninth inning were the blows that won the game, 5–3.

Then the Yankees' Tom Sturdevant yielded but six hits in the fourth game, featured by another Mantle home run and a long home run by Hank Bauer off Carl Erskine that gave the Yanks a 6–2 win.

The fifth game was a classic, one the experts call the greatest game ever in any World Series. Pitcher Don Larsen, traded to the Yankees in 1955 did not walk a man, nor did he allow a hit as the Yankees won, 2–0.

As Larsen continued to mow down the Dodgers, tension mounted

Above left: Yankee sluggers in 1956. In the World Series against the Dodgers this trio of great hitters — Hank Bauer, Mickey Mantle, and Bill Skowron — all hit home runs. Bauer hit one, Mantle slugged three, and Bill Skowron hit a bases-filled shot as the Yankees went on to again defeat the Dodgers and win the World Championship.

Above right: The fifth game of the 1956 World Series was a classic. In the greatest Series game ever played, Don Larsen pitched a perfect no-hit, no-run game to give the Yankees a 2-0 victory.

This remarkable photo tells the story of the fifth game of the 1956 World Series. Don Larsen is shown hurling himself into baseball immortality.

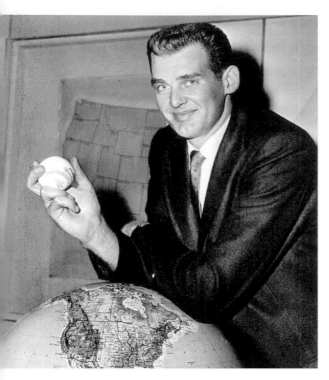

as the innings rolled by, holding the fans silent save when each batter was retired by Larsen. In the ninth inning it was almost unbearable, and Larsen alone seemed impervious to it.

Carl Furillo led off and flied to Bauer, who made a fine catch in right center field. Then Campanella was thrown out by Martin on a great play.

Now with only one out standing between Larsen and a niche in the Hall of Fame, Dodger manager Walt Alston sent Dale Mitchell, a hard-hitting outfielder, up to hit for Maglie. With one ball and two strikes on him, Mitchell fouled off two pitches. Then Larsen, tiring a bit, fired another fastball, and Mitchell took the pitch. But umpire Babe Pinelli, back of the plate, threw up his right hand for a called STRIKE THREE!

Yogi Berra was the first player to reach Larsen, hurling himself at the big pitcher in a bearlike embrace. Before Don could reach the safety of the tunnel leading to the clubhouse, he was mauled, pummeled, hauled, shoved, and stepped on, so that it was wondrous he survived.

Back to Ebbets Field went the two teams for an expected quick finish. The Dodgers could never revive their spirits after the perfect game. But the experts and the Yankees had not considered the tenacity and courage of Clem Labine. Clem had a long way to go, for he had drawn Bullet Bob Turley as his opponent, and Turley was as tough and as game as Clem.

Yankee pitcher Don Larsen holds the ball he used in the final inning of his perfect game in the 1956 World Series against the Dodgers. Larsen turned down an offer of $5,000 for the ball.

Yogi Berra holds a bronzed replica of the glove he used in catching Don Larsen's perfect game in the 1956 World Series.

For ten incredible innings, neither pitcher allowed a run. Then in the Dodger half of the eleventh, with Junior Gilliam on second base, Jackie Robinson lined to left center. It seemed that Enos Slaughter would catch the ball, but at the last moment it took off, went over his head, and Gilliam raced home for the only run of the game.

In the press box, Joe DiMaggio said, "Did you see what I just saw? It looked as if the ball took a bad hop."

But Labine's last stand and Turley's ill fortune—he'd struck out eleven batters and allowed but four hits—merely seemed to delay the inevitable.

The seventh game opened with Johnny Kucks pitching against Newcombe. But big Newk didn't stay around very long. Yogi hit him for home runs in the first and second innings; Elston Howard slugged another homer, and Newk was gone. Moose Skowron hit a home run with bases full off Roger Craig in the seventh inning, and the Yankees had the Series wrapped up like a Christmas gift. The score was 9–0.

And Mickey Mantle, with offers from radio programs and guest appearances at banquets and dinners, was off and back in Commerce two days after the World Series.

All Mickey wanted to do was visit with his wife and children, take them to Commerce High's football games, and just hunt and fish with the boys at his leisure. And he wanted so badly to rest his weary and injured arms, shoulders, and knees all winter long.

Yankee catcher Yogi Berra (8) is greeted by his teammates as he returns to the bench after belting a second homer, in the third inning of the seventh and final 1956 World Series game at Ebbets Field, on October 10. The blow also scored Billy Martin and gave Yogi a new World Series record of 10 runs batted in in a Series. The previous record was nine, by Lou Gehrig in the 1928 Series.

NEW YORK YANKEES
1956 WORLD CHAMPIONS

The Yankees defeated the Dodgers in seven furious games to become the 1956 World Champions.

Clockwise: After the hectic 1956 season had ended, Mickey Mantle received offers for all kinds of appearances, but first he wanted to visit with his wife and children back in Commerce, and rest his weary, injury-laden body.

Mickey was crowned "Tops in Sports" in a huge banquet held in Baltimore on January 15, 1957. In the photo Mickey winks at photographers.

After visiting friends in Commerce, Mickey drops by the local Town Hall pool room and shoots a couple of games of 21.

When the weather permitted, Mickey played some golf with friends in nearby Miami, Oklahoma.

On January 31, 1957, Mickey Mantle received the award presented by the nation's Sports Broadcasters' Association in New York City. Before the dinner, (L-R) Mantle with Frank Gifford, Jim Graham, Tom Courtney, and Sal Maglie.

"During the winter of 1956, since I won so many awards and had such a good season, I started to get a slew of offers for personal appearances," said Mickey. "Frank Scott was my agent and he did a helluva job. After I was at home a couple of weeks I made after-dinner speeches, signed autographs, appeared at shopping malls, and attended banquets in New York, Detroit, Chicago, Kansas City, Cleveland, and television commercials. I even did a record date with Teresa Brewer, producing a song, 'I Love Mickey.'

"It got so that relatives who I never remembered would come up to the house and ask me to do this and that, and it always cost me money in the end.

"One day a fellow named Bill Bankston talked me into opening a big bowling alley in a Dallas shopping center. This fellow outlined the business. 'Mick, bowling is the new rage, the fastest-growing indoor sport of all time, and this is an opportunity to get in on real money.'

The new Mantle family home in Dallas. It was a far cry from the tiny house the Mantles lived in for some years in Commerce.

"So we sold our house in Commerce, bought a beauty of a place in Dallas, packed all our belongings, and made the move into a beautiful ranch house. I took the bowling alley space at a rental of $2,300 per month and got people to put the alley in good condition, and with my brothers, Ray, Roy, and Butch, and other family members working there, I figured that was enough protection that I didn't have to worry about watching everybody every minute of the day.

"Things were looking very good, and everybody had a job.

"Then in January 1957, I went to New York to negotiate a new contract.

"I had proved beyond a shadow of a doubt by winning the Triple Crown that the Yankees should double my salary. But I also remembered that I had trouble with George Weiss almost every year, including my very first season. Weiss wanted to give me $6,000 in 1951, but Casey Stengel talked him into giving me $7,500. And that bothered Weiss. He never forgot it.

"The next year, 1952, I got $10,000. From there I moved up a notch to $12,500, then up to $17,000. But I always had to work out the final details with Weiss's assistant, Lee MacPhail.

"In 1956 I had settled for $32,500 and now, just before the 1957 season with all those honors and awards, I wanted to double that figure. But in my meeting with Weiss, he pulled out a couple of secret reports— a detective report about Billy Martin and me carrying on at all-night parties. Stuff that covered my moves on and off the field. Finally I said the hell with this and started to leave his office and I did.

"The next day I got a phone call from Del Webb, who said he would handle everything, and if I joined him in Florida at the Yankees' training camp, everything would be worked out to my satisfaction. Webb sent

Above left: This was the scene early in the winter of 1957 as Mickey Mantle signed his new contract. Standing behind Mickey, Lee MacPhail, Casey Stengel (L), and George Weiss form a somber trio around their great star.

Above right: "Never in my wildest dreams did I ever figure I would be able to earn this amount of money playing baseball," said Mickey after signing a $65,000 deal for 1957.

Tom Greenwade to pick me up, and we flew to St. Petersburg together.

"I met Del Webb and in a couple of hours I had my contract for $65,000. And never in my wildest dreams did I ever think I would reach that stage. It was more money than I thought existed. It was almost too much."

Remembering the man who had made this all possible, Mickey spoke wistfully about his dad, Mutt Mantle. "Here I am with a lot of money," Mick said, "the kind of dough Dad never dreamed I could get. He thought $10,000 was a fortune. Here I am now with all this fortune and more to come. I could do a lot of things for Dad now, but he isn't around. Just think how I feel about that."

15

ALL THE INJURIES

Now it was 1957 as Mickey reported for spring training in near perfect condition, notwithstanding all the running around, the banquets, dinners, meetings all over the country, and even taking a tour with Bob Hope's television show to, of all places, Alaska. But Mickey was in good shape; for a change, there were no injuries.

Watching Mickey hit his usual long-distance drives in the spring exhibition games, Stengel became enthusiastic.

"One of these days," Casey said, "he'll hit the ball so hard, it'll burst and all he'll get for his efforts will be a single."

Mickey did injure himself as the team headed north. First he sprained a thumb so badly, he could hardly grip the bat. Then while chasing a fly ball, he stepped into a gopher hole and sprained his left ankle. He limped around the rest of the spring season, but by Opening Day, he was once again in tip-top condition.

Just as the team headed north, George Weiss made a deal with Kansas City for pitcher Bobby Shantz. Casey had always liked the looks of Shantz. "He reminds me of Whitey Ford," said Casey, "a little smaller, but a solid pitcher."

Tony Kubek, off the Milwaukee sandlots, a fine infielder, had spent the previous summer in Denver and was a solid performer. Kubek's dad had been an outfielder in the American Association. Kubek could play any position and play it well. Another addition was Bobby Richardson,

Bobby Richardson, who hailed from Sumter, South Carolina, became one of Mickey Mantle's closest friends. A fine, smooth-working infielder, Bobby combined with Tony Kubek to give the Yankees a top-notch second-base-shortstop combination for a number of years.

In an important game against the White Sox on July 23, 1957, Mantle hit a single, double, triple, and won the game with an inside-the-park home run. As Mickey rounded third base, fans poured out of the stands to escort him home. This was the first time since 1952 that an American League player had hit for the cycle.

from Sumter, South Carolina. Richardson could play any position in the infield and play it well.

Otherwise the Yankees were set up pretty much as they had been at the close of the 1956 campaign.

As the season began, the White Sox jumped off by winning several games to take the American League lead, but on May 5 the Yankees caught them in a doubleheader in Chicago and took both games, with Shantz and Johnny Kucks pitching. After that double win over the Sox, all the experts took it for granted that the Yankees would again win the pennant.

Then on the night of May 16, the Yankees created headlines, but not on the sports pages. It was Billy Martin's birthday, and he was guest of honor at a party hosted by Mickey, Whitey Ford, and Yogi Berra. (See Chapter 12 for more on this).

On July 23, the Yankees met the White Sox, who were in second place, on the heels of the Yankees. As the game began, Mantle slashed out a two-base hit. In the third inning, he singled. In the fifth inning, he came up to hit with the bases empty. Batting left-handed, Mickey hit one of the longest home runs into the right-field bleachers. After the game, the drive was measured and it showed that the ball was hit 465 feet. "It was," said Mickey, "one of the hardest-hit balls of my career."

But the game wasn't over. With a double, single, and home run behind him, Mickey came to bat with the bases full and the score 6–6.

Batting right-handed, Mickey slugged the ball to left field. Minnie Minoso tried to catch the drive, but the ball took off and rolled to the fence. By the time the ball was retrieved, Mickey had cleared the bases and was on third for a triple. Mickey had hit for the cycle—single, double, triple, and home run. This was the first time since 1952 that an American League player had hit for the cycle.

By the end of August, Mickey was still very much in contention for the Triple Crown. If he could win the batting, home-run, and runs-batted-in titles for a second year, it would be an unprecedented feat. Mickey hit his 34th home run on August 30. And he was batting .358. The problem was Ted Williams. The thirty-eight-year-old Splendid Splinter was having one of his greatest years.

But as the season waned, Mickey's driving hits did not come as often, and Williams gradually pulled away from him. When a three-game series with the Yankees ended, Williams had a 21-point advantage over Mickey. Williams was hitting an amazing .388. Mantle finished second with a .367 average, highest of his career.

This time the Yankees' perennial World Series rivals, the Dodgers, couldn't make it. The Milwaukee Braves won the National League flag, and great was the excitement as the World Series opened at Yankee Stadium.

Clockwise: Whitey Ford closed down the Milwaukee Braves in the opening game of the 1957 World Series with four hits as the Yankees won the game, 3-1. Here is Bobby Richardson presenting Whitey with the "top hat," indicating the winning hurler.

The Yankees traded Lew Burdette, a smart curveball artist, in 1955. Two years later, Burdette, now with the Milwaukee Braves, allowed the Yankees just two runs and seven hits in defeating them, 4-2, in the second game of the 1957 World Series. In the photo, Burdette is surrounded by his delighted teammates.

In the sixth game of the 1958 Series, the Yankees' second baseman, Gil McDougald, raced to his right to take the final out in the tenth inning. The fly ball was hit by pinch hitter Frank Torres. The Yankees won the game by a 4-3 margin with a two-run rally in the tenth inning. The win tied the Series at 3-3.

For the Yankees, it was the gamer Whitey Ford who was in his greatest form as he allowed the Braves just five hits while Warren Spahn was knocked out of the box in the sixth inning as the Yankees won, 3–1.

The Braves came right back in game two to win, 4–2, as Lew Burdette pitched a fine game for them.

In the first inning of the third game, Mickey was on second base when pitcher Bob Buhl tried to pick him off. Buhl wheeled and threw the ball into center field, but in trying to make the play at second base, Red Schoendienst fell heavily on Mickey's right shoulder.

The shoulder started to pain as Mickey went out onto the field. But he played on. He singled in the third inning. In the fourth inning, he came up to the plate batting left-handed and slugged a gigantic home run.

Mantle played in the fourth game but could hardly swing the bat. The pain was now intense, and he sat out the fifth and sixth games. In the seventh game, Casey inserted Mickey to give the team some life, but a single was all he could deliver. But that was not enough as the Braves defeated the Yankees to become World Champions.

Mantle's average performance in the Series was a thing of memory a couple of weeks later, when it was announced that Mickey was named the

During a play at second base in the third game of the Yankees-Braves World Series in 1957, Red Schoendienst fell on Mickey's shoulder so hard, he had to leave the game. However, injured as he was, Mickey singled and hit a homer in the third game, but it was not enough. The Braves took the Series in seven games.

MVP (Most Valuable Player) in the American League for the second successive year. Neither Joe DiMaggio nor Ted Williams had ever won the MVP twice in succession.

Despite all his aching miseries, Mickey felt wonderful about winning the MVP. He was now the greatest star in the game and one of the greatest attractions in baseball.

"In 1957 the sportswriters voted me the MVP Award for the second consecutive year, but that didn't seem to mean anything to George Weiss," said Mantle. "He sent me a contract that called for a cut of $5,000 from my '57 contract. To Weiss, it seemed I had a bad year.

"I was mad as hell, sent the contract back, unsigned, and said I wasn't going to report unless I got a raise.

"A couple of weeks passed and then I spotted a story in one of the New York papers that stated 'George Weiss said he would trade Mantle if he didn't report immediately.'

"I got on the next plane and was in St. Petersburg in a couple of hours. I met with Weiss and actually got an increase of $5,000, which gave me a $75,000 deal for the season."

But as spring training got under way, Mickey was faced with health problems. His legs, perennial problems, ached like hell, with every start and sudden stop. His right knee had to be taped with rolls of bandages. His right shoulder, injured in the World Series when Red Schoendienst

Mantle's winning his second successive MVP Award in 1957 meant little to general manager George Weiss as he sent Mantle a contract that called for a $5,000 cut. Mantle sent the contract back, then after a couple of weeks, flew to meet with Weiss. The meeting with Weiss produced a raise to $75,000. Mickey is shown all smiles with his new contract.

As spring training got under way in 1958, Mickey was faced with a series of injuries that never seemed to heal. His arm, shoulder, and bad knee all constantly ached. He could not run, could hardly swing a bat, and was unable to play in the early exhibition games. Mickey watches his teammates as he reflects on the injuries that were keeping him out of action.

  THE ILLUSTRATED HISTORY OF MICKEY MANTLE

fell on it, prevented him from swinging a bat from the left side. All in all, he pained with every move.

When the exhibition games began, Mickey could hardly hit the ball with a full swing, and he struck out often. When his below-average hitting continued, sportswriters began to write about Mantle's poor spring showing.

Still Mickey did not complain or talk to Casey about his aches and pains, and as the season opened, Mickey's woes continued.

He didn't hit a home run for a few days, then connected with some good drives. He didn't hit his fifth home run until two months of the season had gone by,

With his battered joints, Mickey began taking diathermy treatments suggested by a specialist. A crippled Mantle is shown with brothers Ray and Roy after a treatment.

Art Ditmar was acquired in 1957 in a five-man trade with Kansas City. Before the season was over, Art had won eight games, all vital in the pennant race.

on June 2. Then he began to feel better, and his home run output began.

Mantle hit his sixth home run on June 4 with two men on base, his seventh homer on June 5, and the next day an inside-the-park home run. Four home runs in five days, and everybody, including Casey and Mickey, began to feel better.

Then, as the pennant race began in earnest, the pace became more intense and Mickey finally had to complain. His knee and shoulder were now giving him such pain that he could not swing at all.

He visited a specialist in Cleveland and began to take diathermy treatments. And once again he turned down all suggestions that he bat only right-handed.

"I was brought up to bat both ways," said Mickey. "I don't see how I can learn some other way."

Going into June, the Yankees spurted, and by June 26 their won-and-lost record was 25–6. Strong pitching by Whitey Ford, Art Ditmar, and Bob Turley were winning games, and the Yankees seemed on their way to another pennant.

Despite all the aches and pain Mickey had gone through, he was not having a bad season. By late August he had lifted his batting average to an even .300, and his home-run output increased.

At one period in August, the Yankees were running away from the rest of the field and led the pack by as many as 17 games. But they went into a slump and won only 25 of their last 44 games. But it was enough to win the pennant.

On the final day of the season, Mickey hit singles in four times at bat to give him a regular-season average of .304. He also slugged 42 home

Bob Turley, a great fastball pitcher. In 1958 "Bullet Bob" was to win 21 games for the Yankees.

The Yankees acquired two pitchers from the Baltimore Orioles in a five-man trade. Don Larsen went on to fame and everlasting glory with his perfect game in the 1956 Series, and Bob Turley was the star of the 1958 Series.

runs, his second-best total as a Yankee. He drove in 97 runs, more than any other Yankee. But he also struck out 120 times.

In the World Series, again against the Milwaukee Braves, Whitey Ford and Warren Spahn dueled each other in the first game, which was tied, 3–3, in the tenth inning. Billy Bruton, the Braves' fine outfielder who had been out much of the 1957 season with injuries, slammed a fastball by relief pitcher Ryne Duren to right field. The ball sailed between Mantle and Bauer for the big run that gave the Braves the game, 4–3.

In the second game Mickey stepped up to bat against an old rival, Lew Burdette. The crafty pitcher yelled to his teammates, "Watch out, he might try a drag bunt down the line."

Mickey laughed, then slugged the first pitch over the fence. His next time at bat, Burdette called out, "Look out, he might drag bunt this time."

This time Mickey slugged the ball over the right-field fence with a man on base, laughing his way all around the bases.

Those were the only home runs Mickey hit in the Series and he ended with a .250 batting average, with six hits in 24 at-bats.

But the Yankees, after being down three games to one in the Series, managed a great comeback by winning the last three from the Braves to once again emerge as the World Champions.

"In my first fourteen years with the Yankees," said Mantle, "we won twelve pennants and seven World Series. The New York fans expected us to win. I guess we spoiled them. In all the years, not once did we get a hero's welcome or a ticker tape parade."

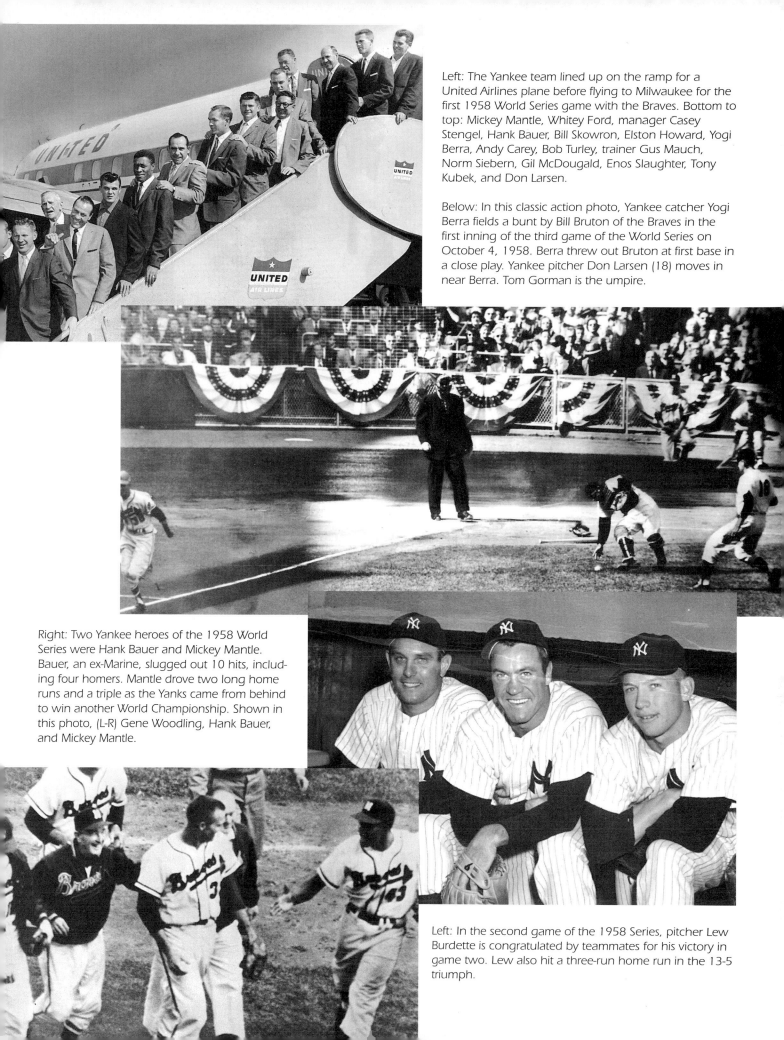

Left: The Yankee team lined up on the ramp for a United Airlines plane before flying to Milwaukee for the first 1958 World Series game with the Braves. Bottom to top: Mickey Mantle, Whitey Ford, manager Casey Stengel, Hank Bauer, Bill Skowron, Elston Howard, Yogi Berra, Andy Carey, Bob Turley, trainer Gus Mauch, Norm Siebern, Gil McDougald, Enos Slaughter, Tony Kubek, and Don Larsen.

Below: In this classic action photo, Yankee catcher Yogi Berra fields a bunt by Bill Bruton of the Braves in the first inning of the third game of the World Series on October 4, 1958. Berra threw out Bruton at first base in a close play. Yankee pitcher Don Larsen (18) moves in near Berra. Tom Gorman is the umpire.

Right: Two Yankee heroes of the 1958 World Series were Hank Bauer and Mickey Mantle. Bauer, an ex-Marine, slugged out 10 hits, including four homers. Mantle drove two long home runs and a triple as the Yanks came from behind to win another World Championship. Shown in this photo, (L-R) Gene Woodling, Hank Bauer, and Mickey Mantle.

Left: In the second game of the 1958 Series, pitcher Lew Burdette is congratulated by teammates for his victory in game two. Lew also hit a three-run home run in the 13-5 triumph.

Right: Mickey wedges out of trouble at the fourth hole as Commerce fans watch him with interest.

Below: "Just as soon as I got home I played some golf, went fishing, but couldn't wait for Thanksgiving to go hunting," said Mantle. In the photo, Mantle with a couple of Commerce pals, Joe Hankins (L) and Jack Maier. The trio caught thirty-eight bass.

CEDAR REST

A happy Mickey Mantle holds up four fingers and a photo of the newest addition to his family, a fourth son.

"It was the same thing in 1958. There was no citywide celebration. I didn't mind. I just wanted to pack my bag and head out home to the wide-open spaces.

"As soon as I got home, I hung around with the family for a few days and went to a half a dozen bars with some local pals. But I couldn't wait for Thanksgiving. That's the time I went hunting with my great friend, Harold Youngman. Even just to be with him was great. I never cared if I didn't shoot a deer or some quail. But when Billy Martin started coming down for the holidays, we took him along with us.

"It meant five days of camping in rocky territory, about fifty miles from San Antonio. We had an old beat-up Ford, and we covered a lot of ground looking for deer. For days we drove and drove and saw nothing much to shoot. But we had lots of fun cooking our meals outdoors and then we had to go back home to face the real world," said Mickey.

"My wife had checked into the hospital the day I left for the hunting trip with Billy, but I didn't think she was sick. So I went anyway," said Mickey.

"Then I got the news from the hospital: My third son was born in the hospital at Joplin, and I hurried back.

"I came to Merlyn's bedside and apologized for not staying with her. Then she smiled and said, 'Okay.'"

"Did you pick a name yet?" Mickey asked.

"Of course. I named him Billy, after Billy Martin."

"I bent down and kissed her. Billy will be happy. I know that for a certainty."

16

Downhill to
Third Place

Spring arrived in 1959, and millions of young Americans threw out
their backs spinning hula hoops. President Eisenhower continued
to ignore all Soviet pleas for trade agreements and talks, and rebel
leader Fidel Castro had driven down from the mountains of Cuba and
begun his final campaign to drive President Fulgencio Batista out of
office with a whirlwind raid against Havana on New Year's Day.

There was great dissension among the members of the Yankee front
office in 1959. Owner Dan Topping decided to eliminate the instructional
school, much to Casey Stengel's unhappiness. Topping also decided to cut
players' salaries.

When spring training opened, a number of Yankee stars, including
Whitey Ford and Mickey Mantle, were unsigned, and a number of others
signed their contracts but were resentful.

Casey Stengel, now 69 years of age, almost didn't come back. But
the lure of winning a tenth pennant and tying John McGraw's record
became too great. But Casey was not in good physical condition that
spring, and began to doze off on the bench during doubleheaders. And it
bothered him that he did not have his usual strength. He was also
annoyed that Topping was losing confidence in him, and he began to
drink and carry on like he did as a young player—so much so that
Topping informed Edna Stengel in California and asked her to come to

In 1959 Casey Stengel almost didn't come back to the Yankees. Owner Dan Topping began to reduce player salaries, Ford and Mantle refused to sign their contracts and Casey himself thought of quitting. Topping contacted Casey's wife, asking her to come to New York and take Casey in tow. Edna Stengel did just that, and from the moment she arrived in town, Casey was "good as gold." In the photo, Edna Stengel kisses her favorite player at a formal dinner in New York.

St. Petersburg to keep an eye on him. She did, and Casey quickly calmed down.

As the season began, the Yankees were beset by injuries on the field and in the bullpen and doubt in the front office. And on May 20 they all came together in a startling headline over a photo showing an unhappy Mantle, his head down. "The Day the Yankees Hit the Bottom," it read.

For the first time since May 1940 the Yankees were mired in last place in the American League, 8 1/2 games behind Cleveland.

On that day, pitcher Frank Lary, the foremost Yankee-killer of his day, had beaten the Yanks, 13–6, and Mickey Mantle had been booed even while circling the bases after a home run.

All through this dismal season, with Mantle injuring his bad knees, his shoulder, and out of action for days at a time; Whitey Ford unhappy at his new contract and not up to his old winning form; Hank Bauer batting in 39 runs; and Andy Carey and Gil McDougald down with the "flu" the Yankees would stagger and stumble through game after game, losing some, winning a few, looking nothing like a contending team.

Then all of a sudden the Yankees started their move.

Led by a revived Mickey Mantle, a healthy Moose Skowron, Hector Lopez, and a brilliant Ryne Duren, who pitched 36 scoreless innings over an 18-game period, the Yankees closed to within 2 1/2 games of the leading White Sox. Mantle, once more hurting, limping, reached down within himself and began to slug the ball in every ballpark. Mickey increased his batting average by some 50 points in eleven days.

But the White Sox could not be denied. In a series against the Yankees, the Sox took three of four games. Then the Yankees lost six games to the Red Sox and dropped to fifth place, 7 1/2 games behind the leading White Sox.

Following the Red Sox series, the Yankees sustained a series of

Mantle tries special exercises for his shoulder, lifting and rotating the arm with a sandbag. But a specialist warned Mickey that he ought to have an operation.

injuries that crippled the team and led to their dismal finish. Mantle jammed his right ankle in a game. This injury, plus his sore shoulder and bad knees, had him hobbling about like a hopscotch player. He was on the bench. Gil McDougald and Tony Kubek collided chasing a fly ball, and both players were hurt on the play. They rode the bench for several days. Finally, their great bullpen stopper Ryne Duren tripped over a cable line on the sidelines, broke his wrist, and was never again able to regain his unbeatable form. And so the Yankees stumbled through to finish in third place.

"I'd like to forget the 1959 season altogether," said Mickey. "The whole year seemed to be full of all kinds of mishaps to me and to a number of Yankees."

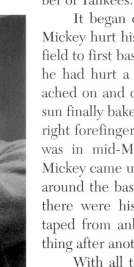

It began on April 12, just before Opening Day. Mickey hurt his shoulder making a throw from center field to first base. It was the same shoulder (right) that he had hurt a couple of seasons back. The shoulder ached on and off until late in July, when the summer sun finally baked it out. Then he chipped a bone in his right forefinger and could not grip the bat firmly. This was in mid-May. Then just when it seemed okay, Mickey came up lame with a sprained ankle, sweeping around the bases after slugging out a long drive. And there were his legs, always aching, that had to be taped from ankle to hip for every game. It was one thing after another.

With all those injuries, Mickey and the Yankees got off to a slow start, and on May 20 the Yankees fell into last place. Nothing like that had ever happened to a Yankee team led by Casey Stengel . . . *nothing*.

Mickey shows Billy Martin just where his shoulder hurts. It's the same injury that occurred a couple of years ago in a World Series play. "It's never healed," Mickey said to his best friend.

"I don't like to say this," said Al Lopez, manager of the White Sox and one of the most perceptive minds in the game, after watching Mickey hit in a couple of games. "I think Mickey is on his way down. I don't think he'll last very long, what with all his injuries."

Shortly after these statements by Lopez, Mickey had the pleasure of driving out a tape-measure home run against the White Sox. The ball landed ten rows deep into the upper deck of Yankee Stadium. "It was one of the best drives I've had in the last two years," said Mickey.

Then early in June, in a game against the Orioles, Mickey struck out three straight times. But the very next day he started on a hitting streak. In seven games he hit for a .522 average. On another day, he managed to come up with five straight hits and another long homer and was fielding his position as well as he ever did.

It wasn't Mickey who was responsible for the Yankees' poor play. It was the fact that several of the other key Yankee players were also suffering at the plate.

During the latter weeks of July and August, Mickey picked up his own hitting, slugging out his 23rd, 24th, and 25th home runs as the Yankees responded by winning several games in succession and rose to fifth place.

But the Yankees were able to go only two notches higher, as they finished the season in third place in the American League.

Mantle finished the season with a .285 batting average, slugged 31 home runs, and drove in 75 runs.

"As the White Sox went into the World Series against the Dodgers, I went home to Dallas bitterly disappointed over the Yankees' third-place finish," said Mickey. "The only pleasing thing was in knowing that I topped the league in fielding percentage."

The trouble with a downhill slide is trying to break it. That's the toughest thing in the world. Mickey's downhill slide began in 1958, after midseason, and it almost paralleled the downhill slide of the Yankees as a team.

Between August 1958 and June 1960, the Yankees lost 120 of 239 games. Then they put on the brakes.

And so did Mickey Mantle.

In December 1959 general manager George Weiss completed a blockbuster trade with Kansas City. It was the fifth in a succession of trades over the past few years with Kansas City, and it involved seven leading players. The Yankees shipped 37-year-old ex-Marine hero Hank Bauer, pitcher Don Larsen, Norm Siebern, and Marv Throneberry to Kansas City and received Joe DeMaestri, Kent Hadley, and outfielder Roger Maris.

"Though I had lost a couple of very good friends in that trade," said Mantle, "I consider myself lucky to find a new good friend in Roger Maris. He came to the Yankees after a few years with the Cleveland Indians and Kansas City. In 1957 Roger was in the running for Rookie of the Year honors when he broke two ribs sliding into third base. After recovering from that injury, Maris became unhappy when the Indians platooned him with

In December 1959 general manager George Weiss made one of the biggest trades in Yankee history with the Kansas City A's. Traded were veteran Hank Bauer, Don Larsen, Norm Siebern, and Marv Throneberry. In return the Yankees received Kent Hadley, Joe DeMaestri, and Roger Maris. And within six months, along with Mantle, Berra, and Skowron, the Yankees had the most potent home-run quartet in recent baseball history. Photo shows Mantle showing Maris his favorite Louisville Slugger bat.

Roger Maris as a schoolboy athlete. Photo shows team picture of Fargo American Legion Junior baseball team in 1950, the year the club won the state championship. Roger is third from left in front row. His brother Rudy is second from left in back row.

Rocky Colavito. Roger was traded to Kansas City, where he began to play regularly. In 1958 and 1959 Maris played under Harry Craft, a fine manager, who had handled Mantle early in Mickey's minor-league career. And it was under Craft that Maris began to hit home runs.

"Maris came to the Yankees a virtual unknown," said Mantle, "but I had seen him play in 1957, his rookie year. He had a great arm, hit savage line drives, and could roam the outfield with great speed."

"Sometimes after a game I'd meet Craft at his hotel room," said Mickey. "We'd talk baseball, then go down to the bar and talk more baseball. Harry would mention certain players around the league. And I clearly remember a night when he said that Maris would hit a lot of home runs if he would ever play for the Yankees.

"'The Stadium is tailor-made for him. Hell, it's only 296 feet down the right-field line. With his ability to pull the ball, he'd have a picnic.'

"My instinct told me that Harry Craft knew what he'd been talking about. And he laughed and said, 'It's one thing to speculate, but the fact is, we want Roger in Kansas City. He could be another Mantle.'"

Still, there were other Yankee questions. Would Moose Skowron recover from his broken arm? Should Tony Kubek play short or the outfield? Who would play third base from among Andy Carey, Hector Lopez, Clete Boyer, or Gil McDougald, a ten-year veteran? And what about the injured arms of Whitey Ford and Bob Turley? Were any of the young pitchers ready to step into the rotation and *win*?

Clockwise: The Yankees had been looking for a successor to the late Lou Gehrig at first base. Bill Skowron had been knocking on the door of greatness for a couple of seasons, but suffered a broken arm in 1958. Now, in 1959, he looked like the Yankees' answer to a powerful hitter, and a fine-fielding first sacker.

Gil McDougald (L) and Andy Carey (R), who will compete for the third-base post in 1960.

Whitey Ford has no pugilistic ambitions. He's merely following the doctor's advice to do some punching exercises to strengthen his pitching arm for the 1960 season.

Despite the big questions, the biggest was Mantle.

Late in December Mickey received his contract, and when he saw that Weiss was asking him to take a $17,000 cut, one that would put him back to $65,000, Mickey was outraged.

Mickey thought he had incorrectly read the agreement. But when he looked at it a second and a third time, he sent it back to Weiss. Weiss said it was no mistake. "That's what you're worth."

It was like a slap in the face, and Mickey became a serious, determined holdout. When spring training officially began on March 1, Mickey was nowhere to be seen.

A few days passed, and suddenly Mickey found it impossible to be away from baseball and his pals, who were already working out at St. Petersburg. He flew down to St. Pete and immediately went into a lengthy discussion with Weiss. When it was finally over, Mickey came out with a solemn face.

He faced the press: "They gave me a pretty stiff cut," he said. He donned his old uniform and offered, "I'm surprised my number wasn't trimmed from number 7 to 6 1/2."

The biggest question mark for the Yankees in 1960 was Mickey Mantle. He was not happy at all after his salary squabble with George Weiss. Mickey was enraged when Weiss cut Mantle's 1960 contract some $17,000. Here's Mantle emerging after a two-hour battle for a better deal.

In spring training as the exhibition games began, the Yankees looked bad, and as the season began, they continued to slump, alongside their leader, Mantle, for Mickey was locked in the worst slump of his career.

The Yankees lost 20 of their first 41 games as they waited for Mickey to round into shape to lead them out of their fifth-place position in the league.

In early June, with Casey Stengel in the hospital with a severe virus that slowed him to a walk, Ralph Houk was named acting manager. Houk shook up the lineup by giving Johnny Blanchard a chance to catch. Hector Lopez was in left field, and Clete Boyer was at third base.

Then the Yankees played the defending league-champion White Sox in a four-game series. They lost the first game as Whitey Ford gamely tried for a win. But three costly errors by Mcdougald cost them the game. Then a marvelous four-hit game by Jim Coates, another brilliant game by Turley, and Ralph Terry with a great game and the Yankees came away from that series with three wins. Mantle was superb in each of the games, slugging four big home runs, a couple of singles, and a double. The Yankees seemingly were on the road to the top.

When Stengel returned with this statement: "The docs in the hospital examined all of my organs. Some of them are quite remarkable," he croaked, "others are not so good. A couple of museums are bidding for them." That broke up the entire team, and suddenly with Casey back in charge, the Yankees won eight straight games. They lost a game, then streaked for six more in a row, including the four-game sweep of the White Sox.

Now the Yankees were in first place.

One thing that seemed to be helping Mantle as he hit several home runs against Cleveland and Kansas City was the presence of Roger Maris in the lineup. Maris was batting in the fourth spot and was taking a good deal of pressure off Mickey, batting third. With Mantle, Maris, Berra, and Skowron batting in that order, opposing pitchers had to pitch carefully, for these four were all potential home-run hitters.

In a game against the Tigers, Mickey hit two consecutive home runs off Frank Lary. When Maris came up to hit after Mickey, Lary became ruffled and walked Maris both times.

Just a day after Mantle hit the homers off Lary, Mickey complained to the Yankee trainer

Above: As he returned from the hospital in June of 1960, Casey Stengel has some words of wisdom for his ace pitcher, Whitey Ford. "I wasn't sick, I just wanted to rest for a while," said Stengel.

Left: Now in 1960, with a batting order that included Mickey Mantle batting third, Roger Maris fourth, Yogi Berra fifth, and Moose Skowron sixth, the Yankees had their own version of "Murderers' Row."

about his bad right knee. "It hurts like hell, worse than last year," said Mickey. "I think all the ligaments are torn."

Still smarting and badly hurt by George Weiss's treatment of him, cutting his contract by nearly $10,000, Mickey felt that after nine years of service he should have been dealt with on a different basis. He couldn't forget this, and it had happened with Weiss every year since 1951.

With his bad knee and his attitude against Weiss, Mickey began to be careless on the field. In one game he struck out and stepped back into the dugout, not realizing that the ball had skipped by the catcher and he could have reached first base. Another time Mickey was on first base and dashed for second on a routine fly ball and he was doubled off the base. Later he said, "I thought it was two outs."

In an important game on August 13 against the Senators, and with Maris on first base, Mickey hit a ground ball and simply failed to run it out. The Senators again made a double play. Mickey again said he thought there were two outs.

Then in a white-hot rage, Stengel pulled Mickey out of center field and inserted Bob Cerv in his place.

It was a moment of deep humiliation as the big crowd hooted Mickey for his lapse.

Later Stengel cooled down and said, "He don't stop running because he's lazy. He gets mad at himself because he isn't hitting the ball good. And then he goes into the dugout and starts kicking things around. It's a bad habit. He's got to get rid of it, for the good of the club and for himself."

A contrite Mantle, determined to atone for his poor judgment in the past few games, began to drive the ball out of the ball park.

In a game against the Orioles, as Mickey's name was announced at bat, the Stadium crowd booed him. As he grounded out weakly and as he continued into the dugout the catcalls continued.

In the fourth inning, Mickey came up to hit with Hector Lopez on base and drove out a long home run to tie the score. In the eighth inning, again with Lopez on base, Mickey hit one into the bleachers for a home run that won the game and put the Yankees back into first place. Now the Stadium was alive with cheers, and as Mickey stepped into the dugout, he raised his cap to the crowd in a salute.

The Yankees revitalized, and sparked by Mickey's return to his old form, began to chalk up victories. They won the last 15 games of the season to win the pennant. Whitey Ford won his final three starts. Ralph Terry allowed just two runs in 22 innings of pitching, including a memorable pennant-winning game against the Red Sox on September 25. Stengel said, "Terry, you look like Walter Johnson in the stretch. You were one of the best I've ever seen."

Rookie Bill Stafford pitched 19 innings during that final drive and allowed but three runs, and Bullet Bob Turley, after a disastrous start at

Pitching played a vital part in the Yankees' great stretch run in 1960, when the Yanks won their last 15 games of the season. In the photo, Roger Maris talks with pitcher Ralph Terry, who allowed just two runs in his final 22 innings of pitching, including the pennant-winning game against the Red Sox.

the beginning of the year, made a marvelous comeback to end with a 9–3 regular season.

From famine to feast, the spotty Yankee pitching corps suddenly became one of the hottest in the league. This was the foundation of great things to come in the next few years.

And Mickey Mantle led the league with 40 home runs. Roger Maris slugged 39 homers to give the Yankees an incredible one-two home-run punch that was the scourge of opposing pitchers. Twenty of Mickey's home runs had either won games or set up wins. Mickey led the league in runs scored with 119.

In the drive to win the pennant in 1960, the Yankees were led by Mickey Mantle and Roger Maris, who slugged a total of 79 home runs. Maris hit 39 homers, while Mantle hit 40. Twenty of Mickey's home runs had either won games or set up wins.

"It's amazing what he has done this year," said Stengel. "And him a cripple, playing on one leg. He's twice as good a fielder as he was last year. Nobody, and I mean nobody, like him I've ever seen." This from Casey after a wondrous catch by Mantle in a game against the Red Sox late in the 1960 season.

And now a happy Casey Stengel let himself go in evaluating Mantle.

"It's amazing what he has done," Casey said, "and him a cripple playing on one leg. He's twice as good a fielder this year as he ever was last year. The wind or anything else doesn't bother him, and he chases every ball and like a big rabbit gets them. And he has hit the big home run in the late innings of second games and doubleheaders and it's a good thing I don't take him out for a rest in second games, or we'd lose a lot of games. Nobody like him I've ever seen."

In the National League the Pittsburgh Pirates won their first pennant since 1927, the year Babe Ruth and Lou Gehrig crushed them in four straight games. Stengel also reminded everybody he had played for the Pirates in 1918 and 1919, before any of his ballplayers were born.

The 1960 World Series opened in a carnival atmosphere at Forbes Field in Pittsburgh, a town completely covered by "Beat 'Em, Bucs" signs. The ballpark itself was a league antique that opened in 1909, but it was intimate and colorful, with dimensions approaching those of Yankee Stadium: a short distance to the right-field fence, and 435 feet to the fence in straightaway center field.

Casey was faced with a number of problems going into this World Series. He was unsure who to pitch in the opening game, and he was mistrustful of his "green peas," such as Richardson, Clete Boyer, Hector Lopez, and Bill Stafford. All the coaches—Ralph Houk, Ed Lopat, and Frank Crosetti—agreed to withhold Ford until the teams returned to New York for the third game because of Whitey's unbeatable record at Yankee Stadium, but disagreement arose as to who would start the first game. Eddie Lopat, the pitching coach, pushed hard for rookie Bill Stafford. "This kid is the closest to Whitey Ford," said Lopat over and over. Casey agreed, but Houk and Crosetti were adamantly opposed to starting a rookie in the first game. They felt that Art Ditmar should start. Finally, Ditmar got the assignment, and he faced the Pirate ace, Vern Law. Ditmar never got beyond the first inning.

In the top of the first inning, Roger Maris slugged a home run. But the Pirates came back as Bill Virdon, their center fielder, walked and got to third base on a wild throw by Yogi Berra. Dick Groat then singled past Richardson. The Pirates picked up two additional runs and went on to win, 6–4.

In the second game it was all Mickey Mantle. He drove out two massive home runs as the Yankees slaughtered the Pirates, 16–3. Mickey continued his hitting in the third game as he singled his first time up, singled in the second inning, and in the fourth inning blasted a gigantic 430-foot home run into the left-field bullpen. In the fifth inning Mickey got his fifth hit, a ground-rule double into the stands. And the Yankees once again clobbered the Pirates, this time 10–0.

Before the fifth game of the 1960 Series, these three Pirate stars are smiling. (L-R) Harvey Haddix, starting pitcher in game five; pitcher Vernon Law in the middle; and captain Dick Groat on the right. After the game, which the Bucs won, 5-2, all the Pirates were smiling.

Hitless in the fourth and fifth games, Mantle drove in two runs with another single as the Pirates won both games.

The sixth game was another rout for the Yankees as they clobbered the Pirates, 12–0, behind Whitey Ford.

In the seventh game the Pirates jumped to a 2–0 lead as Vern Law seemed unhittable. Then it was 4–1 in the sixth inning, but the Yanks weren't through.

Bobby Richardson singled to start the sixth inning. Kubek walked, Maris fouled out, but then Mantle fired a savage single, scoring

Left: Mickey Mantle was a terror at bat in the second game of the 1960 World Series. Mickey slugged two home runs, a triple, a double, and two singles for a five-hit assault as the Yankees clobbered the Pirates, 16-3. In the Series, Mickey hit for a .400 batting average, got 10 hits, scored eight runs and drove in 11 runs, and hit three of the longest home runs in World Series history. In the photo, Mickey holds three bats for his three home runs.

Below: Yogi Berra, bat in hand, rushes out of the dugout to congratulate Roger Maris on his home run in the second inning of the fifth game of the 1960 Series. Yogi also hit a home run, with two men on base, in the seventh game. But the Pirates won the game and the Series.

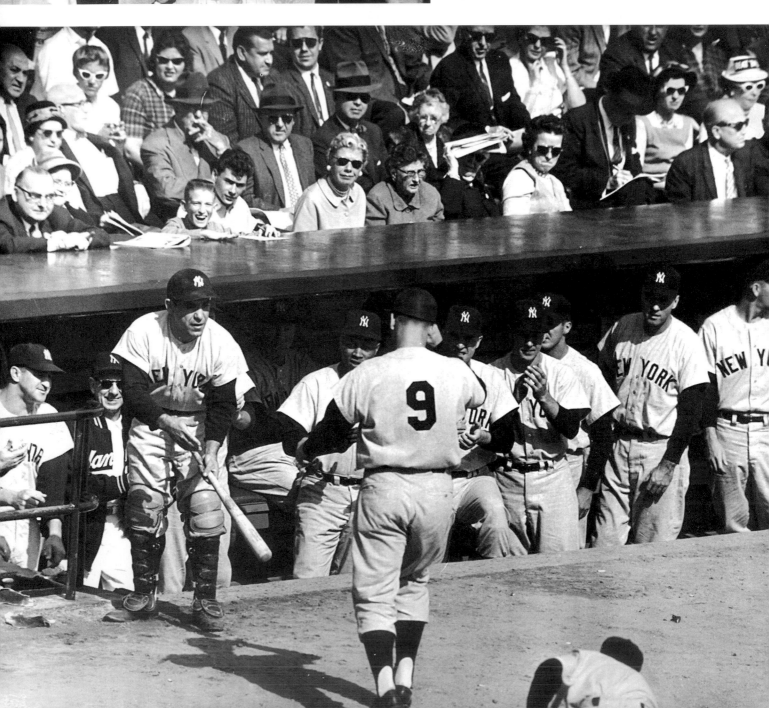

Rubber-armed Roy Face appeared in four games as a relief pitcher for the Pirates in the 1960 Series and saved three games. This great action sequence shows Face's form as he saved the fifth game, which the Pirates won, 5-2.

Richardson. Then Yogi came up and drilled a three-run homer and now the score was 5–4, New York.

In the top of the seventh the Yanks scored two more runs, making it 7–4. But catcher Hal Smith hit a home run with two men on base, and two more runs came in, giving the Pirates a 9–7 lead.

In the top of the ninth inning, the Yankees got two men on base, and Mantle lined a single to left to make it a 9–8 game with Pittsburgh on top. Then on a play that should have ended the inning and the Series, Mantle, on a double-play ball, eluded the tag, allowing McDougald to score to tie the game at 9–9.

But in the bottom of the ninth inning, with the score still 9–9, second baseman Bill Mazeroski picked out a fastball by Ralph Terry and smashed out a home run to give Pittsburgh their first World Championship since 1925. The city had the biggest demonstration in its history.

And Mickey Mantle? What happened to him after the game?

Mickey was hunched down in the locker room, tears streaming down his cheeks. He was crushed.

"This is the first time we ever lost a Series," he sobbed, "that we should have won."

But it hadn't been Mantle's fault. He had his best World Series, batting .400, with 10 for 25. He scored eight runs, drove in 11, and hit three of the longest home runs in history.

17

A NEW YANKEE MANAGER

Two days after the 1960 World Series, Dan Topping conducted a press conference at the Savoy Hotel in New York. Casey Stengel agreed to attend the conference, one conference that would announce his retirement as manager of the Yankees. A retirement that Stengel fought tooth and nail.

"He was seventy years old," said Topping, "and we have to make a change . . . a change that we had delayed for a couple of years."

After Casey read the prepared statement that was to go to the press, he spoke his mind: "Look, fellas, I'm not about to retire. I was fired. No matter what Topping says, I was fired after giving the Yankees the greatest winning record of ten World Series. That's a world record. I was plain fired and I'm damn mad."

The angry barrage of the sportswriters filled the room, and there were all kinds of angry remarks directed at Topping and Del Webb.

Topping took all the criticism and said, "Twelve years ago, when we first hired Stengel, we were ridiculed. Today when Casey is leaving, we are ridiculed again. But it's time for a change, and we have to make it now."

On November 2, 1960, the other shoe dropped. Like Stengel before him, George Weiss, who had guided all of the behind-the-scenes administrative duties of the Yankees, was "retired." But unlike Stengel, Weiss agreed that it was time for him to leave.

"I was not happy to see Casey leave the Yankees," said Mantle. "He had been great to me, more like another father. It was Casey who brought me up to the Yankees in 1951, at least a year before the upstairs management thought I was ready. It was Casey who helped my dad, Mutt, realize his dream, seeing me as a major leaguer. It was his dream before he died. Casey taught me a great deal about baseball, and he helped me through some of the worst spots of my life. His patience was endless. I did get sore at him a few times, as any player gets sore at a good manager. But it really saddened me to see him leave.

"But I was delighted to have Ralph Houk get the job. Ralph was a man like my old manager in the minors, Harry Craft . . . a man you could respect . . . a man who made you want to win. A fellow who hated to lose, just as much as I did."

Ralph Houk had been an aspiring rookie catcher in the Yankees' farm system for a few years, including a year at Joplin, where he hit a solid .319. (Joplin was also the team Mantle played with, in 1949.)

Houk then enlisted in the Army, was sent overseas, and was in the great Battle of the Bulge. It was here that the Nazis began their last significant counteroffensive, with a force of 250,000 men and 1,000 tanks. And it was here that Lieutenant Ralph Houk, with some sixty handpicked Rangers, began to harass a company of Germans.

Lieutenant Houk's military record speaks for itself:

"Deliberately exposing himself to the withering fire of the Germans, Houk calmly moved from one post to another, directing his men, battering the enemy with machine-gun fire. Taking over a tank destroyer, Lieutenant Houk personally directed the fire against the enemy, forcing them to retire from a vital area. He then led his tank destroyer to knock out the lead German tanks, stalling the enemy's attack."

The official record went on. "Later on, for continued acts of heroism, Lieutenant Houk was awarded the Silver Star, the Bronze Star with Oak Leaf Clusters, and in quick order was promoted to first lieutenant, captain, and major. . . ."

This, then, was Ralph Houk, the Yankees' new manager. And when Houk arrived in St. Petersburg for the Yankees' spring training in 1961, it was readily apparent that there was a new, exuberant spirit among the players. Under Houk the players felt a greater sense of security. Ralph did not believe in shifting players from position to position and did not like platooning.

In the first week at St. Petersburg, Houk announced that Bobby Richardson and Tony Kubek would be his second-base and shortstop combination; Ellie Howard, his catcher; and Yogi Berra, Hector Lopez, and Mickey Mantle would be his outfield.

He also announced that his pitchers would pitch every fourth day and that the Yankees would win the pennant.

"A few days after taking over the team I talked with Mickey and told him how much the other players admired him and that I'm counting on him to be the leader this year," said Ralph Houk. "With you out there every day," said Ralph, "we can't lose."

A few days later, Houk announced that Mickey Mantle would be the leader of the team. "I talked this over with Mickey," said Houk, "I told him how much he meant to the team, and I told him that the other players look to him, and with him we can't lose."

In turn, Mantle reported to spring training several days before the rest of the squad and promised Houk 100 percent cooperation. Mickey said he was looking forward to his best year.

Five of Mickey Mantle's most avid fans read a United Press International dispatch telling of Mickey's selection as the American League's Most Valuable Player for the 1962 season — the third time he won the honor. The fans are David, Mrs. Mantle, Dan, Mickey, Jr., and Billy in the rear.

Mick really felt that way this year. It had been a good winter. He had been less involved in business ventures than ever before and even stayed at home with Merlyn and the kids.

He had disposed of his big Dallas bowling alley, which had cost him a small fortune, had closed out other various interests, had cut down on appearances, and said, "Right now I'm concentrating on the business of winning another pennant."

And for the first time there was little hassle with management on his contract. He got a $10,000 increase, which now gave him his best Yankee contract, at $75,000.

"Mickey Mantle should have a big year," Ralph Houk told reporters who were on hand for the opening game of the season, and Mickey was eager to do just that.

"Let's get going!" yelled Mantle to his teammates as they dashed out onto the field for the opening game of the season. But pitcher Whitey Ford didn't have much on the ball and was battered in a 6–0 loss in that first game.

The next day it was better as the Yankees won, 5–3 and Mantle homered. In the next four games against the Orioles, Mantle homered in each game. The Yanks took four straight, and Ralph Houk was beginning to look good.

  THE ILLUSTRATED HISTORY OF MICKEY MANTLE

18

HOME-RUN DERBY

The Yankees won ten of their first fourteen games in 1961, and seven of them were decided by Mickey Mantle's big bat. He drove out eight home runs six of them decisive blows that won ball games. Now he was leading the league in home runs, and he was fielding in spectacular fashion.

On April 17 Mickey hit a two-run homer and went 3 for 4 as the Yankees won, 3–0.

On April 24 Mantle hit a 390-foot home run to give Whitey Ford a 4–2 win.

On April 26 the Yankees faced the Tigers, who had won ten games in a row and looked like world beaters. The Yankees scored five runs in the first inning and another run in the second to make it a 6–0 game. But the fighting Tigers came right back on a home run by Rocky Colavito, two singles, and a double, plus a wild throw by Ellie Howard. By the seventh inning it was a knock-down, drag-'em-out battle as the Tigers erupted for five more runs to go ahead, 11–8.

In the eighth inning, Richardson singled. Kubek doubled him home. Then Mantle slugged out a long homer to tie the score at 11–11. The game went into the tenth inning, when Lopez singled. Then Mickey stepped up to hit and on the first pitch slugged a long home run that gave the Yankees the hard-fought game, 13–11.

On May 2 Mantle drove a low pitch by Camilo

Mickey visits with his mother during the Christmas season in 1960 in a new home he purchased for her.

In 1961 Mickey Mantle, with the added responsibility of being the Yankees' leader on the field, quickly began his home-run slugging. By early May Mickey had hit his 12th homer. Roger Maris, spurred on by Mantle's batting, began to find the range and by May had hit 11 homers. By early June, Maris had 20 home runs and Mantle had hit 18, and it began to look as if Mantle and Maris were in a race.

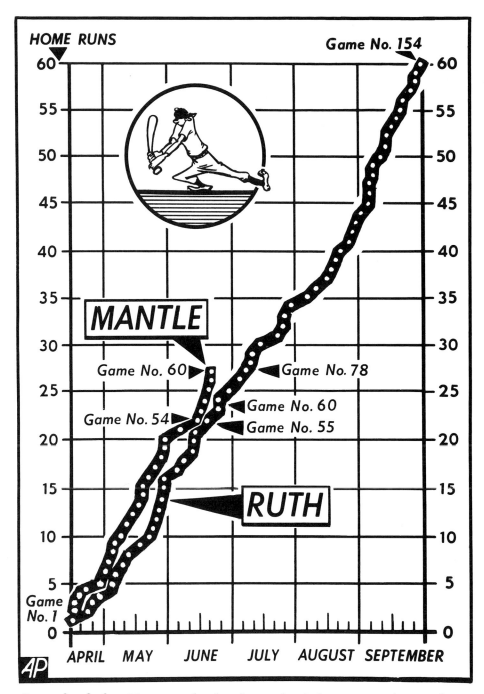

HOME RUNS

Game No. 154

MANTLE

Game No. 60 ▶ ◀ Game No. 78

Game No. 54 ▶ ◀ Game No. 60
◀ Game No. 55

RUTH

Game No. 1

APRIL   MAY   JUNE   JULY   AUGUST   SEPTEMBER

Dots in the rising black lines represent home runs hit by New York Yankee slugger Mickey Mantle so far in 1961 and Babe Ruth's record 60-homer spree in 1927. Mantle hit his 26th and 27th round-trippers in his team's 60th game on June 20, putting him 18 games ahead of his Yankee predecessor. Ruth didn't smash his 27th homer until July 8, but finished strong, with 17 home runs in September.

Pascual of the Twins with the bases loaded to give the Yankees another extra-inning win, 6–4. This was Mickey's sixth grand slam of his career.

Roger Maris had started slowly, but by the end of May both Maris and Mantle were hammering the hell out of the ball, driving enemy pitchers to cover. If the pitchers got Mantle, Maris would drive the ball out of the park. If they got Maris, Mantle would slug a home run.

By May 30 Mantle had hit his twelfth and thirteenth home runs of the season, and Maris wasn't too far behind. In Boston, both Maris and Mantle hit home runs. Now it was 13 homers for Mantle, 11 for Maris.

By June 12 Mickey had walloped 18 round-trippers, while Roger Maris had slugged 20. By July 1 it was 28 for Maris. Mickey hit two home runs that day against Washington to give him 27 homers.

Now, this was a race. . . .

The Mantle-Maris home-run race was soon to overshadow every other race in both major leagues, including the drives for the pennant. This was a home-run derby that had fans all over the country talking about it.

On July 25 Maris slammed four home runs in four games against the White Sox to give him a total of 40 homers. Suddenly everybody was talking about Maris challenging Babe Ruth's great home run total of 60 in a season. Maris was 24 games ahead of Ruth's schedule. But Mantle was right on Maris's heels, with 38 home runs. Mickey was 20 games ahead of Ruth's schedule.

Everything in baseball took second place as Maris and Mantle kept up their tremendous slugging. Who would top Ruth's record? Would it be Maris? Would it be Mantle?

On July 26 Mickey drove out home run 39. Now he was just one home run behind Maris.

Was 1961 the year that two men would break Ruth's great record?

"Will it be you or Maris?" Dick Young of New York's *Daily News* asked Mantle.

Mickey always turned the conversation to other things, but this time he answered, "All Roger has to do to tie Ruth's record is to hit 10 homers in August and 10 in September, and the way he is going he should do that without too much trouble."

It was always that way with Mickey. Turn the talk to the other guy's chances. When Maris nosed Mickey out for the MVP Award in 1960, Mickey said, "Roger deserved it. Didn't he carry the Yankees for more than half the season with his big bat?"

Mickey moved ahead of Maris by driving out a home run against Washington on August 13. Then Maris followed suit by hitting two homers. Now they were tied on August 15, with 45 each.

Sports editors were now beginning a special "home run" box in their daily columns, and fans continued to talk about the home-run derby in their every baseball discussions.

There was never anything like it in the long history of the major leagues. Everywhere Mickey and Roger went, the sportswriters were after them, the fans were after their autographs at breakfast, lunch, or dinner. They took to sneaking out the back doors of their hotels. They took strange routes to get to their apartments.

Mickey, Roger, and Bob Cerv were now sharing an apartment in

The Yankees' home-run sluggers Roger Maris and Mickey Mantle were selected to play in the annual All-Star game at San Francisco on July 11. Maris at this time had hit 33 homers while Mantle had 29. Mantle batted third in the All-Star lineup, while Maris hit in the fourth spot. The photo shows the two stars awaiting their turn in batting practice at Yankee Stadium before leaving for San Francisco.

Mantle connected for one homer August 13 in the first game of a twin bill against the Washington Senators in Washington. Maris hit one in each game. They stand tied at 45 each, 15 games ahead of the pace set by Ruth when he set the record.

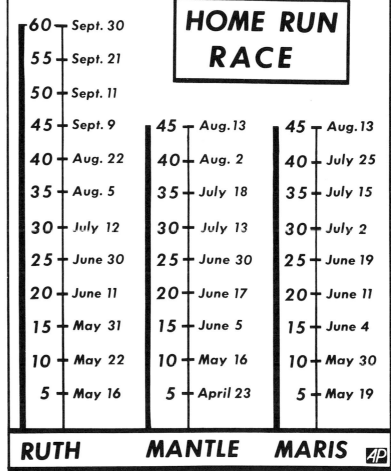

HOME RUN RACE

RUTH		MANTLE		MARIS	
60	Sept. 30				
55	Sept. 21				
50	Sept. 11				
45	Sept. 9	45	Aug. 13	45	Aug. 13
40	Aug. 22	40	Aug. 2	40	July 25
35	Aug. 5	35	July 18	35	July 15
30	July 12	30	July 13	30	July 2
25	June 30	25	June 30	25	June 19
20	June 11	20	June 17	20	June 11
15	May 31	15	June 5	15	June 4
10	May 22	10	May 16	10	May 30
5	May 16	5	April 23	5	May 19

Queens, and one day after Maris had hit a homer, Cerv shouted, "That's the way to hit 'em, roomie!"

"Thanks, Bob," said Maris. "When we get back to the apartment, remind me to show you something."

That night, back in their Queens hideout, Maris walked into the bathroom and called to Cerv. "I want to show you what's happening since the home-run thing began."

As the home-run derby became the biggest sports story of the year, Mantle and Maris took a small apartment with Bob Cerv to get away from the press hounding their every minute. "And despite the great rivalry in the home-run race," said Cerv, "Mickey and Roger were good friends. It was most unusual."

Cerv walked in and Maris said, "Look at this stuff."

Roger took off his shirt, and his arms, shoulders, and chest were covered with goose bumps. The same kind of bumps that kids get when something really excites them. The home-run derby had done this to Maris.

"Jeez, Rog, have you shown this to our team doctor?"

"No," Roger said. "I don't want any pills or injections right now. We're in a tough pennant race, and this derby is just another thing in the race. I'll just have to bear with it until we finish the season."

"It got to be routine after that," said Cerv. "Every time Maris hit a couple into the seats he broke out with those bumps. It was scary. I don't know how he lived with all that, the newspapermen, fans, and just everybody pestering him night and day.

"I told him one night he ought to work out a way of having the goose bumps before he went up to hit. It would have knocked off a lot of the tension and pressure that built up for him during that famous stretch run in September.

"I learned a lot about pressure and its relationship to ballplayers," said Cerv, "during my four months of sharing an apartment with Mickey Mantle and Roger Maris in the Richmond Hill section of Queens in New York in the summer of 1961. And I also learned a lot about Mickey Mantle and Maris. You have to learn things about people when you live with them almost every day in a 3 1/2-room apartment. You see them in the morning before they've had a chance to mellow over a cup of coffee. You see them at the ballpark, you play the game with them, and then you see them at night when maybe they're trying to forget they had a bad day.

"This, of course, was a unique arrangement. I'll bet there's never been anything like it in the history of baseball.

"Here were two fellows in competition for the biggest prize in baseball, attempting to break Babe Ruth's home-run record, and here they were sharing an apartment—with me.

"When this great home-run derby really started to cook up along about the beginning of August, I told myself it would either bring out the worst in them, or the best. I am happy to say the whole experience made bigger men out of Mantle and Maris.

"These are my sentiments. Forget all the honors, the extra money involved, the personal sense of accomplishment they both must have felt. Wherever I am in the years to come, I'm going to remember one thing about rooming with Mickey and Roger in 1961. I think I can express myself best by way of a little poem an old grammar school teacher taught me many years ago. It went like this:

> Be careful of the words you speak . . .
> Keep them soft and sweet;
> For you never know from day to day
> Which ones you'll have to eat.

"Roger and Mickey never had to eat any words they bandied about in that apartment in Queens, but if they had, they wouldn't have choked on any of them. They may have been great rivals in that incredible home-run race, but they were smart enough to let their bats talk for them. They never once got into any kind of hassle around the house.

"Take the matter of cooking breakfast, for instance. With the exception of an occasional steak or after-game snack, breakfast was the only meal we had in the apartment. At first we tried to think of a system that would let every fellow cook for everybody else. It would be my turn one morning, then Mickey's, then Roger's. That worked one or two times. Then we knocked it off.

"I'll put it this way. Mickey and Roger may have been the hottest home-run hitting combination in the history of baseball, but they were absolutely the worst cooks in Queens County.

"Now, they may have felt the same way about me, and we decided that each of us would do his own cooking. That way if anybody got poisoned he'd have nobody to blame but himself. So I'd cook my bacon and eggs sunny-side up, Mickey would cook his easy over, and Maris would do his well done. Once we got that little problem settled, things moved along fine. You have no idea what trouble you can get into fooling around with food for hungry ballplayers.

"Overall, it was really wonderful, though, how well our apartment worked out. We hadn't planned on it, and the three of us had never roomed together before. Roger and I had, but not with Mickey.

"Life in the apartment wasn't fun and games with a lot of bright chatter. Mickey and Roger seemed to get their kicks out of just lounging around in the quietest way possible. There'd be some nights in that apartment where you wouldn't hear a word spoken for an hour or more.

"But starting about the middle of August, as each of my roommates were hitting all those home runs, there wasn't a day when some newspaper editor or sports commentator didn't ask if he could send someone out to the apartment to do a story on how the three of us lived together. The answer was always the same: NO. And we never regretted it."

"How're your legs holding out, Mickey?" asked Dick Young as Mickey limped into the dressing room after slugging a towering home-run late in August.

"Okay," said Mickey, although it was not true. His legs and back were giving him trouble, slowing him down. "But don't count on me. I don't want to think about Ruth's record. I'm just concerned with the team's record. But if anybody breaks the record, it will be Maris."

On September 2 Mickey hit his 48th homer. Now he was five behind Maris. What was worse. Mickey had pulled a muscle in his right arm and could barely swing his bat. By September 13, however, Mickey had begun to close the gap. He had 50 home runs, just 3 behind Maris.

The headlines now read, "Maris 57, Mantle 53" on September 29, when Mickey was ordered to the hospital.

He had a high temperature, was very weak, and it was discovered that his right hip, injured in a collision, was infected. He was out of the home-run race and out for the rest of the year. Nevertheless, he led the league in slugging percentage, with .687.

Roger Maris went on to pound home runs. He got his 58 and 59, then tied Ruth's great record of 60. In game 154, the last of the regular season, Maris slugged a pitch by Tracy Stallard of the Red Sox for home run 61, and Babe Ruth's record was broken.

As Roger trotted around the bases, the entire Yankee team came out of the dugout to shake his hand and to hug him. And the big crowd rose in their seats to cheer him for five minutes. It was a tumultuous scene, a

Opposite page: "How are your legs holding out?" asked Dick Young, New York Daily News sports editor. Mickey had just hit his 48th home run. "Not too bad," said Mantle. "But don't count on me breaking Ruth's record. It will be Maris." In truth, Mantle's legs, knee, and shoulder ached so much he could hardly swing a bat. On sheer courage, Mickey hit two more homers to give him a total of 54. Then he was ordered to the hospital after doctors discovered that a hip injured while sliding had become infected and there was a jagged hole that bled every time he swung. Mickey was out of the home-run race and out for the season. Photo shows the pain Mantle suffered each time he hit the ball.

Above: Roger Maris crosses home plate after hitting his 61st homer on October 1, to surpass Babe Ruth's record. Maris connected off right-hander Tracy Stallard in the fourth inning of a game between the Yankees and the Boston Red Sox. Greeting Maris are Yogi Berra (8) and the Yankee batboy.

Right: In the Yankees' clubhouse after Roger Maris had broken Babe Ruth's record, the Yankees celebrate, tearing his shirt off and dousing him with champagne.

record-breaking one for the Yankees and for Roger Maris.

His year's work on the diamond had been done, and what a great year it had been for Yankee superstar Mickey Mantle.

He had banged out 163 hits, 54 giant home runs, and had scored 128 runs. It was indeed a great year. And sportswriters all over the country weren't slow to recognize it.

Roger Maris had electrified the baseball world with his remarkable home-run record, and there was no doubt about his winning the Most Valuable Player Award. Still, so great was the performance of the Oklahoma kid Mickey Mantle that the sportswriters pretty nearly gave that award to the young veteran of the Yankee squad.

There were seven first choices for Roger Maris, six for Mickey Mantle. The final count was Maris 202, Mantle 198.

The Yankees walked away with the pennant in 1961 thanks to

In the race for the coveted MVP in 1961, Roger Maris received 202 votes. In second place was Mickey Mantle, with 198 votes.

Above: In the first game of the 1961
World Series, Whitey Ford, the Yankees'
ace, shut out the Cincinnati Reds, 2-0.
Ford also pitched in the fourth game,
leaving in the sixth inning, but not before
he broke Babe Ruth's World Series record
of 29 2/3 consecutive scoreless innings,
set in 1918. Whitey hurled 33 1/3 consecutive World Series innings in the World
Series from October 8, 1960, to October
4, 1962.

Right: New York Yankee right fielder John
Blanchard slides into home plate and
sends Cincinnati catcher John Edwards
sprawling in the sixth inning of the fifth
game of the World Series. The play came
when Red pitcher Bob Purkey fielded
Hector Lopez' sacrafice bunt and threw
wildly to Edwards, Blanchard scoring.
Yankees won the game, 12-5, and the
Series, 4-1.

Yankee manager Ralph Houk (left in back of player with jacket) runs out to greet his Yankee team as they win the 1961 World Series over the Reds.

The 1961 World Champions New York Yankees

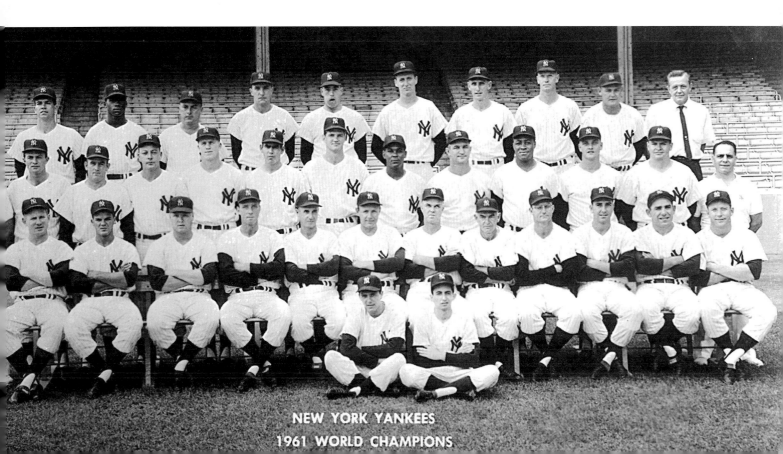

NEW YORK YANKEES
1961 WORLD CHAMPIONS

Mickey Mantle, Roger Maris, and manager Ralph Houk.

"Make me look good," Ralph Houk said to Mickey Mantle in the spring training.

He did.

They also took the World Championship, beating the Cincinnati Reds, four games to one.

The big question in Ralph Houk's mind, and in the minds of all baseball fans and sportswriters as well, was: Can that young eleven-year veteran of the Yanks, the all-time great Mickey Mantle, keep going? And for how long? How long can he last on those ailing legs? Will he be able to play in 1962?

It had been a wonderful winter for Mickey Mantle in 1961. It seemed as though everyone recognized the great change that had come over the thirty-year-old superstar. The pressure of the terrific 1961 home-run duel between Mickey and Roger Maris, the fact that Maris had beaten Babe Ruth's record while Mickey nursed injuries, seemed to have completed the sympathy and understanding for Mickey that had begun late in 1960, when he was pulled out of a game for not running out a drive to the infield. Now Mickey was being accepted for what he was, and that was the heir to Ruth, Gehrig, and DiMaggio.

As the world seemed a more pleasant place for Mickey, he became more pleasant toward the world.

Now the pressure was on Roger Maris, and Mickey could relax more than ever. He hunted back home, played a lot of golf, saw more of his family, and began to earn a good deal of money in deals developed by his agent Frank Scott.

And in 1962 there wasn't any bickering for his new contract, which called for an estimated $82,000, the highest salary of his career.

In spring training Roger Maris and Mantle were still reaping the benefits of the home-run race. Among the deals was a $25,000 guarantee for a motion picture called, Safe at Home! Their part in the picture was shot in three days at the Yankees' spring training camp in Fort Lauderdale. It was produced by Columbia Pictures.

In the spring of 1962, now in his second year as Yankee manager, Ralph Houk brought up a number of new faces, prospective young stars he thought might bring the Yankees another pennant. There was a brash, snappy first baseman, Joe Pepitone, with all the ability in the world if he would settle down. Joe liked a good time and was always ready for fun. Then there was Tom Tresh, a switch-hitter whose dad had been a major-league catcher and who had been brought up from Richmond at the end of the '61 season. Young Jim Bouton came up from the Amarillo team and later became a big-time winner. Pitcher Roland Sheldon, who had been 11–5 for the Yankees in 1961, and Marshall Bridges, acquired from the Reds, bolstered the pitching staff. And Ralph Terry, 16–3 in 1961, returned.

And the veterans were on hand this spring of '62, Whitey Ford, a great 25-game winner in 1961 looked as good and trim as he did in his first year with the Yankees, back in 1950. Roger Maris was ready to hit some more home runs, perhaps break his own record of 61. And most importantly, Mickey Mantle was ready.

And the consensus of most of the sportswriters covering spring training camps was, "If Mantle is not hurt and hits like he can, the Yanks will win again."

Mickey and Roger Maris once again began the 1962 season in rare form and began hammering the ball as the Yankees jumped out in front in the American League.

Above: Joining Mickey Mantle and Roger Maris at the world premiere Columbia's <u>Safe at Home!</u> was actress Tina Louise.

Left: Mickey Mantle shows fellow Yankee stars the brochure for the Mickey Mantle Fund for research in Hodgkins' disease, at a luncheon in New York. Mantle, whose father died of the disease, was chairman of the foundation. (L-R) Mantle; ex-Yankee Billy Martin; Hank Bauer, now with Kansas City; Bill Skowron; Yogi Berra; and Jerry Coleman. All the players, along with fourteen other ballplayers, formed the Foundation Committee.

By May 6 Maris had hit six home runs; Mickey had seven. During one game against Washington, Mickey hit three home runs, one after the other. And it looked as if the Yanks would run away with the pennant.

In a series against the Red Sox in May, Maris leaped high in an attempt to catch a wicked line

Above: During the off-season's in 1961 and 1962 Mickey could hunt, fish, see his family, and play a lot of golf. In the photo Mickey blasts out of a sand trap.

Below: Ralph Houk brought up some new faces for the 1962 spring training camp. (L-R) Jim Bouton, Phil Linz, Tom Tresh, veteran Robin Roberts, Marshall Bridges, Joe Pepitone.

drive in Fenway Park, came down hard, and injured his left leg. He would be out of action for a number of days. A day later, Mantle, running down the first-base line, suddenly fell to the ground. It was so sudden that it almost looked as if Mickey had suffered a heart attack. Upon examination by the Yankees' trainer, it appeared that Mickey's right leg had buckled. After more than five minutes along the first-base line, Mick was able to hobble to the sidelines, assisted by two players.

Mickey was driven to Lenox Hill Hospital, where it was found that a large muscle of his leg had been torn. "It was torn," said the doctor who attended Mickey, "by the sheer force of Mickey's body and the fierce run for first base. And it will take the better part of several weeks of rest and rebuilding before he's ready to play."

Upon his release from the hospital, Mickey could hop about on crutches, then went back to his family in Dallas. There he took daily therapy from Wayne Rudy, a trainer for the Dallas Texans football team.

Meanwhile, the Yankees put up a brave front. "Well, we'll miss him," said Houk, "but we'll just have to play the best we can."

Sportswriters in Dallas visited Mick one day and asked about his leg. "It's coming slowly," he said. Then he pointed to a swelling under his right knee.

"It fills with water," said Mickey, "then it spreads to the knee. See this," he said, pointing to a long scar. "This is where they cut it, to get some of the fluid out."

Early in May in a game against the Senators, Mickey hit three home runs in three successive at-bats as the Yankee swept the series and moved into first place. In the photo Mickey is giving Yogi Berra a face massage, a reward for Berra's home run and double.

In a game against Minnesota early in May, Mickey Mantle drove a liner to right field. In speeding to first base, he suddenly crumpled to the ground. The action was so sudden it looked as if he had suffered a heart attack, and the big crowd was stunned into complete silence. Doctors discovered Mantle had torn a leg muscle, and he would be out of action for weeks.

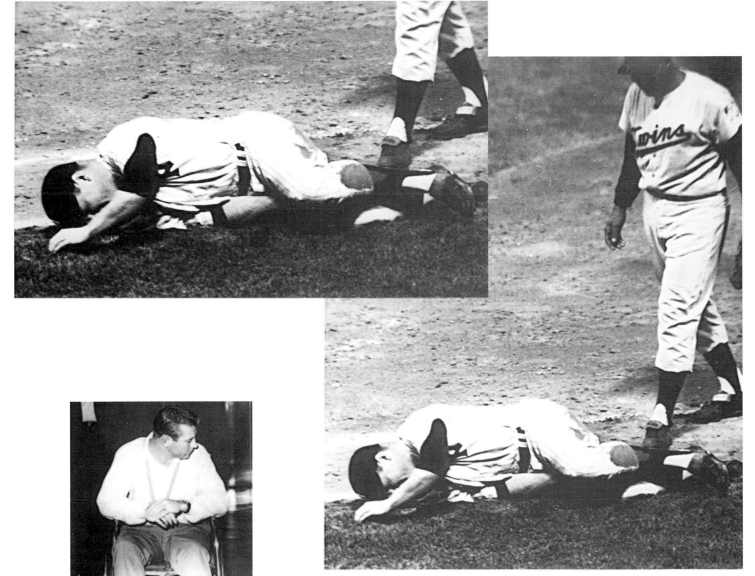

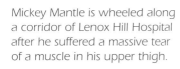

Mickey Mantle is wheeled along a corridor of Lenox Hill Hospital after he suffered a massive tear of a muscle in his upper thigh.

Three weeks after the injury, Mickey got a call from Roy Hamey, the Yankees' general manager. "Mick, we want you to rejoin the team. The guys will feel better with you around, even if you can't play for a while."

"I'll feel better, too," said Mickey.

He met the team in Los Angeles. Bobby Richardson saw him in the hotel lobby and shook his hand. Bobby said, "It's hard to explain, but just seeing him gave me a lift."

Back with the ballclub, Mickey kept pestering Houk to let him play.

"Maybe a couple more weeks, Mickey. It all depends on what the doctors say."

Mickey kept after Houk. Mickey couldn't sit on the sidelines. He had to be on the field with his pals.

But it wasn't until June 13 that Ralph Houk inserted Mantle into the lineup, and then for just six innings.

With Mantle in the lineup, the Yankees played superbly and took two out of three games against Los Angeles to put them into a tie for first place with the Angels.

"Now you guys are on your own," said Mantle. "I got you here in first place, now do the rest yourselves."

It was great to have Mickey around the dugout. But it would be nicer to have him there suiting up ready to take his place on a regular basis in the lineup.

One evening before a night game, Houk suggested that Mickey try to play and he would run stiff-legged. The players laughed, and Mickey led the laughter. "I wish the damn thing would heal already," said Mickey.

Then on June 16, against the league-leading Indians, who were ahead, 7–6, in the eighth inning, two men were on base when Houk called on Mickey.

"Mick, go on up and hit for Bridges. But if you hit it on the ground, don't bother to run. Give 'em the double play."

Mickey didn't hit the ball on the ground. With a 3–2 count he cut into the next pitch and hit it high and far into the stands for a thunderous three-run home run as the Yankees took a 9–7 lead. As Mickey limped around the bases, even Indian fans joined with the Yankees as they roared a tremendous acclaim for this.

Mickey pinch-hit twice more in the next two games. He ground out and struck out. But he was happy: His leg was getting stronger, and the team with its captain back in action, was again in the pennant race.

On June 22, in an important game against the Tigers, Mickey started the game and played the full nine innings. He rapped a double in three at-bats and scored twice. Ellie Howard described the Yankees' response to Mickey's full return: "It was one of the greatest things that could happen to the club. He just picked up the whole team."

At the All-Star break Mickey's batting average was .333. He had 17 home runs, five in the previous eight games. And the Yanks as a team had won 13 and lost five with Mickey in the lineup.

Ralph Houk said, "The reason Mickey's looking so good at the plate is that he's taking those bases on balls. The way it used to be, Mickey would get tired of seeing so many balls and so few strikes and he'd be going after bad pitches to hit."

"It looks like you're out of the woods," said editor Dick Young of the *Daily News*.

"Nothing wrong with me now," Mickey quipped. "But the back is still stiff and it aches after I take a real swing."

On June 29 Mickey hit a home run, then on July 4 he hit two homers. On July 5, he hit another home run. He was back in stride, and no one was happier than Ralph Houk.

Mickey's terrific hitting continued. From July 22 to July 25 the Yankees won-lost record was 22–9. In the previous 17 games Mickey had hit for a .427 average, with 16 RBIs.

"There's no question that he's playing as strong a game as he has ever played," said Ralph Houk. "I've just got my fingers crossed that he doesn't get hurt again. The trouble is that Mickey is so big and strong and plays with fierce abandon that his body can't take the drive. He just doesn't drive into a base, he punishes his body to get to that base, and when he slides, heaven help anybody in his way. I've never ever seen such determination in my life."

Then it happened again.

On August 11, in a game against Cleveland, Mickey's left knee felt so sore that Houk pulled him out of the lineup. He missed eight days. Then with rest and treatment he was ready for the wars once more.

On August 19 Mickey proved that he could still run bases with the best in the game. Against Kansas City Mickey singled in the third inning, then stole second, then third base. In the fifth inning, with the bases full, Mickey slugged out a long home run—a grand slam. In the sixth inning he singled and then stole second base. He left the game in the sixth inning, but his contribution was amazing: a grand-slam home run, double, single, and seven runs driven in as the Yanks swamped the A's, 21–7. It was one of Mantle's greatest individual days.

On September 4, in a tense game with the Tigers, Mickey came up to bat against a tough Tiger pitcher, Hank Aguirre.

On the first pitch, Aguirre, a great curveball artist, fed Mantle his best curve, which looked like it was right on the money. Mickey thought so, too, and drove his bat into the ball with terrific force. The ball took off—higher and higher it went, for one of Mickey's longest home runs, a blast of some 450 feet. It was Mickey's 400th home run, one that he would never forget.

The Yankees went on to best the Tigers, 3–1, and in the dressing room after the game, Mickey was surrounded by sportswriters, friends, and teammates congratulating him on his 400th home run. That put Mantle in seventh place among the all-time home-run batters. Ahead of him were Babe Ruth, 714; Jimmie Foxx, 534; Ted Williams, 521; Mel Ott, 511; Lou Gehrig, 493; and Stan Musial, 460.

After the game someone asked Mickey if he thought that someday he might overtake Musial.

"How old is Stan?" he asked.

"Oh, forty-one or -two," a sportswriter said.

"Tell you one thing," said Mickey, "I'll trade bodies with Stan anytime."

The following three days the Yankees were able to beat off a persistent challenge from the Tigers, whom they defeated, then battered Minnesota and were once again winners of the American League pennant.

And Mickey Mantle, who went through the worst pain he had ever endured as a ballplayer, went on to have one of his greatest seasons.

In the World Series, as so often happens, the big stars were pitchers—in this case Billy O'Dell, Jack Sanford, Billy Pierce, and Juan Marichal of the San Francisco Giants, who stifled the big bats of Mantle,

Above: Mantle is greeted at the plate by Hector Lopez as he scores his twenty-sixth home run of the season in the fifth inning of the game with the Detroit Tigers. It was Mantle's 400th major league home run. He was the seventh player to reach that goal.

Right: Two of baseball's greatest stars met head-on in the 1962 World Series. In the first game, all Willie Mays did was to hit two home runs and a double, and the Giants took the game. Mantle, although aching with a bad knee and a bad back, managed a couple of singles.

Skowron, Maris, and Ellie Howard. In turn, Yankee pitchers Ralph Terry, Whitey Ford, and Bill Stafford held off Willie Mays, Orlando Cepeda, Filipe Alou, and Jim Davenport as the Yankees defeated the Giants in a renewal of their age-old battles. This one went the entire seven games before the Yankees, behind the magnificent pitching of Ralph Terry, who had a no-hit game for six innings, beat the Giants as he kept the great Willie Mays hitless and four-hit the Giants to win the seventh and deciding game. The Yankees once again were the World Champions.

Mickey Mantle did not play too well in the Series, but he could look back on the regular season with great satisfaction.

Missing about a third of the season, Mickey still hit 30 home runs in 123 games and ended the regular season with a .321 batting average.

Mickey didn't win the MVP unanimously. He did receive thirteen of the twenty first-place votes. He was the only player named on all twenty ballots. He finished with 234 votes to 152 votes for the runner-up, Bobby Richardson. It was the most one-sided vote in the league since 1956, when a player named Mantle was the unanimous choice.

After the events of the previous fall and winter, it was most fortunate that in the spring of 1963 there was a spring training session for major-league baseball.

In late October 1962 President Kennedy, alarmed that the Soviets were setting up offensive missile bases in Cuba, ordered a complete quar-

Above Left: Jubilant New York Yankees pitcher Ralph Terry is hoisted on the shoulders of his happy teammates October 16, after pitching a 1-0 win over the San Francisco Giants in the final game of the 1962 World Series in Candlestick Park. The victory gave the Yanks their 20th World Series Championship.

Above right: Although Mickey Mantle missed about one third of the 1962 season because of various injuries, he hit 30 home runs in 123 games, and ended the season with a .321 batting average. Thus it was no surprise that Mickey was voted the MVP Award for the year. Mickey finished with 234 votes to 152 votes for teammate Bobby Richardson.

The Sporting News named Mickey Mantle the top American League player for its All-Star team in 1962. The photo shows three All-Stars with Mantle: (L-R) former Yankee Bob Cerv, Gus Triandos, and Rocky Colavito.

antine of Cuban waters. U.S. Navy warships blockaded the area. Any Soviet ship carrying offensive missiles was to be stopped, boarded, and searched, and if such a ship refused, it was to be blown out of the water. It was like the shoot-out at the O.K. Corral, except that instead of six-guns, if the crisis realized its full potential, each side would be exchanging fifty-megaton bombs.

Fortunately for the whole world, the Soviets decided that having offensive missiles in Cuba wasn't worth having the world destroyed, and Premier Khrushchev turned the Soviets convoy of ships around to avoid a confrontation.

At that, Premier Castro of Cuba called Khrushchev a coward.

At the Yankees' spring training camp in Fort Lauderdale, Ralph Houk predicted that the Yankees could again win the pennant. "Why not?" he reasoned. "We're better than we were last year."

This would be Houk's last year as Yankee manager until 1966, because he finally accepted Roy Hamey's offer to become general manager in 1964. It was a secret shared by Yogi Berra, who was to be a player-coach in '63 and then manager of the Yankees in 1964.

The Sporting News, the bible of major-league events and statistics, named Mickey Mantle the top American League player for its All-Star team in 1962. The Yankee slugger was also awarded the Golden Glove Award as the outstanding outfielder for 1962, and the Baseball Writers' Association of America named Mickey the Most Valuable Player for 1962.

The 1962 World Champion New York Yankees.

NEW YORK YANKEES
1962 WORLD CHAMPIONS

On February 27, 1963, Mickey Mantle signed a new contract, which called for $100,000. Yankee general manager Roy Hamey and former Yankee great Joe DiMaggio, a special coach, looking on.

There seemed to be no end of honors for the former mining messenger from Commerce, Oklahoma, as he went into action in 1963 for his thirteenth season with the Yankees. In his first three games Mickey drove out two home runs, two singles, and a triple, and seemed headed for another glorious year.

Then once again that old injury jinx, which had plagued Mantle from his earliest year with the Yankees, struck again. Making an impossible try for a line drive, Mickey pulled a muscle in his abdomen. That injury, plus one of those disabling spring colds that aggravated the abdominal muscles, kept him on the bench for a few days.

"It's not that bad," said Mantle. "But every time I had to sneeze, I kept hurting my stomach. And I can't swing a bat at all."

Baseball's most famous invalid limbers up on the sidelines before a game against Kansas City. Evidently the warming up by Mickey Mantle was worthwhile, as he hit a home run that won the game in the eleventh inning, one of the longest homers ever seen in Kansas City.

Manager Houk could hardly contain Mantle, and in a few days he was back in action and hitting the ball to distant fences.

By the middle of May the Yankees had taken over first place thanks to Mantle's batting. In a game against Kansas City and with the score tied, Mantle drove a home run in the eleventh inning that won the game. The blast from Mickey's bat cleared the facade of the ballpark. It was the farthest drive ever at Kansas City.

At the crack of the bat, the fans knew that the game was over. But to a person, they got to their feet and watched in awe as the ball disappeared from sight.

"It was one of the longest home runs I've ever hit," said Mickey.

"I've seen most of the great hitters," said Ralph Houk, "but I've never seen a ball hit harder."

In a June 4 game against Baltimore, Mickey had come to bat four times. He had been walked twice, hit a single and a two-base hit, and scored two runners. Everything was going in favor of Mantle and the Yankees. Then an abrupt turn in events and the picture, which had been all sunshine, turned into darkness.

"We had a night game in Los Angeles, to be followed by a double-header in Baltimore," said Mickey, "and all the players were so tired they could hardly hold their heads up. I mean, we got to Baltimore at 4:00 A.M. and had to play two games the next day.

"Then in the first game, Brooks Robinson, the Orioles' great third baseman, slugged a pitch by Whitey Ford and I had to give it my hardest run to get near the ball, and just as I jumped to catch the ball, I cracked hard into the concrete fence that was corded off by some wiring and I came down hard. My foot caught in the wiring and it was twisted so badly, I knew it was a bad injury."

Mickey couldn't get up, and the Yankee trainer, Houk, and Whitey Ford were out there, helping.

A couple of players and the trainer carried him off the field, rushed Mickey to Union Memorial Hospital, and the next day the X rays showed a broken foot.

They had asked Mickey in the spring if he was going to go after the hitting title, the home run crown, the big Triple Crown.

"Do you have any objectives?" sportswriters had asked Mickey at the spring training camp.

"Yes, I have an objective," answered Mickey, smiling all the time. "My objective is to stay in one piece."

Well, he wasn't in one piece.

"I don't think it's as bad as the doctors

Teammates carry New York Yankee outfielder Mickey Mantle off the field on a stretcher in Baltimore on June 5 after he slammed into the fence in a vain bid to catch a homer off the bat of Brooks Robinson in the sixth inning of a game with the Orioles. In attempting the catch, Mantle caught his left foot in the fence and broke a bone. The Yanks won the game, 4-3.

say," Mickey told his worried teammates, but it was bad enough.

By the end of June he was hobbling about on a pair of crutches, and he was far from ready to return to the baseball wars.

He reported to the ballpark, but Ralph Houk urged him to go home.

"You can't run," said the serious manager. "You just get well fast. We need you around here when you're ready to play."

They elected Mickey Mantle to play in the All-Star game, crutches and all. It was a gesture by the ballplayers, the sportswriters, and the fans. Mickey was still sidelined as far as baseball was concerned, but everybody missed the slugger, everybody was cheering for him, and they wanted Mickey to know it.

In the first week of August, Mickey got back into the game as a pinch hitter. It was a magnificent return.

It was one of those wild-scoring games against the Orioles, who were leading, 10–9, in the seventh inning when Mickey was announced as the batter.

The roar of the crowd would be heard on radio and TV in Baltimore and in Washington, as forty thousand fans rocketed their cheers across Yankee Stadium. For more than five minutes they stood and roared his name.

"I figured there'd be a little noise," said Mantle. "But I never figured it would be that big." He shook his blond head in disbelief. "It was nice. It was real nice."

But the initial roar was nothing compared to the one that was soon to follow.

Oriole southpaw George Brunet whipped a fastball across the plate.

"Strike one," growled the umpire behind the plate.

Brunet took his windup, let the ball fly, and Mickey connected with a thwack! And as the fans rose once more from their seats, that ball took off in a high, beautiful arc and sailed over the left-field wall—a smashing home run to tie the score and lead to an eventual win over the Orioles.

The fans roared at the swing of Mickey's bat, and the roaring didn't let up as the great Yankee slowly circled the bases. Still the big crowd couldn't help noticing the manner in which their great hero did his circuit around the diamond. It was obvious that Mickey Mantle still was not fully recovered from his injury.

Mickey, of course, laughed it off.

"My legs are fine now," he said, "but I pulled my ribs on that swing."

It was a joke, but it really wasn't funny. And he said nothing of the loose cartilage outside his left knee. That would need the surgeon's knife, and it was coming soon.

Mickey played in only 65 games in that 1963 season, and went up to bat 172 times, but he banged out 54 hits, 15 of them home runs, and his batting average for the year was .314.

What doesn't show in the record books, however, was the tremen-

His foot in a cast, Mickey Mantle is helped from a private plane of his boss Dan Topping at LaGuardia Airport on June 6. Aiding Mantle is his teammate Whitey Ford. Mantle was flown to New York from Baltimore, where he sustained the broken bone in his foot.

Above: On October 6, 1963, Ellie Howard shakes the hand of
Mickey Mantle after Mickey's home run in the fourth game of
the 1963 World Series. But the Dodgers came back to win the
tense Series finale, 2-1, to sweep the Yankees.

Above right: A quartet of Dodger and Yankee stars engage in
small talk as they oblige photographers at pre-World Series
workouts at Yankee Stadium on October 1, 1963 — pitchers
Sandy Koufax, Don Drysdale, Whitey Ford, and Mickey
Mantle.

Above: Noted actor Walter Matthau is
the Dodgers' official mascot for the
World Series.

Left: Manager Ralph Houk of the
Yankees and Dodger boss Walt Alston
meet to discuss ground rules for the
first game of the 1963 World Series at
Yankee Stadium.

Los Angeles Dodger manager Walt Alston comes up on the dugout steps to welcome catcher Johnny Roseboro after he had crashed a second-inning three-run homer in the first game of the 1963 World Series at Yankee Stadium. Maury Wills shakes Roseboro's hand. Moose Skowron (14) and Dick Tracewski (44), both of whom scored on the homer, trot to the dugout. Clapping hands at left is coach Leo Durocher. The player between Durocher and Alston is Ron Fairly. The Dodgers won, 5-2, as Sandy Koufax struck out 15 Yankees to set a World Series record.

dous lift in morale that the slugger gave his teammates. He was in only 65 games as a player, but he was in every game of the schedule as a Yankee. It was the will of the mighty slugger, his courage, his heart, that constantly inspired his club, and the Yankees came in with the pennant once again, 10½ games ahead of their nearest rival, the Chicago White Sox.

Once more, Mickey had made Ralph Houk look good, as Mickey himself put it: "I was well enough to be able to play a couple of games in the World Series of 1963," said Mantle, "and at least make an effort to help save our hides."

But who could beat Sandy Koufax and Don Drysdale that year?

"In that World Series, they were the best pitchers I had ever seen," said Mantle, "and I counted myself very lucky to get a home run off Sandy and a single off Drysdale, to give me a batting average of my youngest boy's collar. This was the worst beating I had ever seen the Yankees take, four straight beatings, and it left me aching for another crack at the Dodgers. But this was not to be. At least we'll never have to face Koufax again, and that may be a very good thing for everybody's batting average."

It was just after the World Series that Ralph Houk, who had done a masterful job as the Yankee manager, was moved up to Roy Hamey's post as the general manager of the team. In his place, Ralph named one of the great Yankee stars, Yogi Berra, to handle the team in 1964.

Yogi was one of the most unusual men ever to play ball. He was short, muscular, and stocky, and after Bill Dickey worked with him for a couple of seasons, Yogi became one of the great catchers in baseball. He had become sort of a clown with his

Don Drysdale is mobbed by teammates as he left the field after pitching the Dodgers to a 1-0 victory in the third game of the 1963 World Series.

First baseman Joe Pepitone of the Yankees chases the ball in the seventh inning, after letting a throw from teammate Clete Boyer go through him for an error. Jim Gilliam of the Dodgers, who hit the high bounder to Boyer, races all the way to third on the play. The next batter up was Willie Davis, who hit a long sacrifice fly, allowing Gilliam to score easily with the winning run for the Dodgers in their 2-1 victory in the final game of the 1963 World Series.

odd manner of speaking, but all the stories and jokes about Yogi were pure poppycock, for he was one of the smartest men in the game.

When Yogi was growing up in a place called Dago Hill in St. Louis, he lived across the street from Joe Garagiola, who later on became a fine catcher for the Cardinals.

"When we were growing up and playing ball," said Joe, "Yogi was the first guy that we would choose as captain. No matter what the sport was, baseball, football, hockey, or what," said Garagiola, "Yogi knew all the rules, the different plays, and the strategy. He was the smartest guy in any game we played. I remember we were all excited about a hockey game that was being played. And we argued about some player that played years ago. Yogi came back with the whole story of this player, how many years he played, how many goals he scored. Yogi was unbelievable.

"Both of us tried out with the St. Louis Cardinals for a spot as catcher. After the tryouts, both Yogi and I were selected to play with a minor-league team. I got a bonus of $500 to sign a contract," said Joe, "and I told Yogi about it.

"When it came Yogi's turn for a contract, Branch Rickey of the Cardinals offered him $250.

"But Yogi said, 'Mr. Rickey, my pal Joe Garagiola got $500. If I can't get $500, I can't play with your team.'

"Rickey, one of baseball's smartest general managers, said, 'Yogi, I've got just $250 for you. Okay?'

"'No, sir,' said Yogi. 'Five hundred dollars is what I want, or I'll play elsewhere.'"

And that is exactly how the Cardinals lost the services of catcher Yogi Berra, for just $250. A few months later, Yogi was signed by the Yankees and got his $500 bonus and $90 per month to play for Norfolk, a Yankee farm team in the Class B Piedmont League.

19

YOGI BERRA, YANKEE MANAGER

Yankee manager Yogi Berra lined up his club. This was their first meeting in the spring of 1964 at the Fort Lauderdale spring training camp.

He spoke seriously.

"These are my rules," he announced. "No swimming, no golf, no jai alai, no racetracks, no gambling at all."

The faces of all the Yankees fell a mile. Was this the "great guy" Yogi Berra talking? Was this the happiest and funniest fellow the club talking?

Yogi continued.

"Everyone in at eleven-thirty. Lights out at twelve. Turn your radios off, too. Everybody out on the field at seven-thirty in the morning, and everybody better look like a Yankee. Everybody in uniform. No blue jeans. No shorts."

He stopped for a moment, took in his squad.

"That goes for all of you. Except the coaches and the manager. We can do anything we want to do!"

He paused again, looked at all the glum faces, then he let a slow grin come to his mouth, and the squad gave out with a whoop and a holler.

That was the way it was with Yogi as he began to manage the Yankees. He would have to change that style no matter how much it hurt, before the season got very old.

Of course, the big question, in the spring camp was: "How does Mickey shape up?"

Mickey Mantle, shown on crutches early in the 1964 season, is as brittle as he is brilliant. His latest ailment, a knee injury, has shelved him indefinitely. Mantle's illnesses, head to toe, are charted: tonsilectomy, 1956; right shoulder, '57; rib cage injury, '63; abscessed right hip, '61; fractured right index finger, '59; pulled right thigh muscle, '55 and '62; cyst operation behind right knee, '54; sprained left knee, '55; bruised left knee, '62; cartilage operation on right knee, '51; reinjured right knee requiring another operation, '52; osteomyelitis in left ankle and shin, '47; break in metatarsal in left foot, '63. Mantle has been plagued since youth, when he suffered a form of infantile paralysis that weakened his legs.

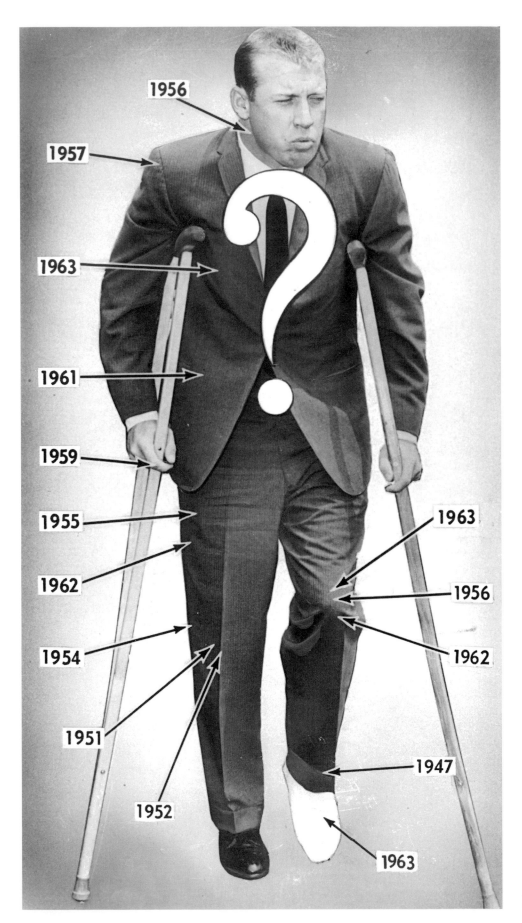

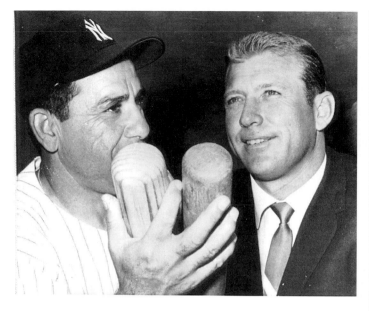

He had gone under the surgeon's knife to have the knee cartilage removed in October, but no one could really say whether the operation had been completely successful.

"You can't know if you can run without a limp until you begin to run every day," said Mickey.

He had played golf during the winter. He had used a weight machine to strengthen the knee. He had run the 100-yard dash at three-quarter speed and been clocked in 11 seconds.

"I've slowed up," he admitted. "I did think of quitting the game last year," he added, "after busting up my rib cage and breaking my foot. But I'm here. I'll try."

He tried, all right, and Yogi had to get after him to slow down.

"You're running too hard," said Yogi. "Take it easy. Please! There's no rush, nobody rushing you. Take it easy!"

But Mickey couldn't take it easy. He didn't know how. And it was Mickey's bat that kept the Yankees up in the first division the first two months of the pennant fight.

On July 4 the Yankees trailed the league-leading Baltimore Orioles by 3 1/2 games, but Mickey's big bat blasted out home runs, keeping the Yankees on the heels of the Orioles.

Mantle hammered out his 17th home run and was leading the Yankee hitters with a .330 batting average, the only Yankee with a better-than-.300 clip to his credit.

On July 15 a typical Mantle homer decided a Yankee win over the Orioles, and the New York club was in first place by half a game.

Above left: Mickey Mantle signed his second consecutive $100,000 contract with the New York Yankees at their spring training camp in 1964. Manager Yogi Berra is looking at Yankees star.

Above right: May 12, 1964: Yogi Berra, New York Yankee manager, celebrating his thirty-ninth birthday today, was presented this birthday cake in an impromptu greeting prior to game with Detroit Tigers.

It was a perilous lead. It didn't last. The Yankees had a real fight on their hands.

This was not going to be a runaway for any club in the American League. Now, late in August, it was the Orioles holding a slim 1 1/2-game lead over the White Sox, with the Yanks five games back of the leader.

Then Mantle returned to the lineup after one more bout with his bad legs, and cracked out a double and a home run to help snap a Yankee losing streak. Then an inspired Yankee team began to move.

"We're not out of the race yet, not by a long shot," said Mickey as he talked to his teammates in the locker room before a game. "It's not gonna be easy. But let's pull ourselves up, give it the old Yankee drive, and win a couple of games."

In a vital series with the Yankees' perennial rival, the Red Sox, Mickey, gimpy legs and all, ripped two home runs in two days as the Yankees moved up a notch in the pennant race.

Yogi Berra reminded the sportswriters, "Remember, the Yanks come on strong," and "We ruined and broke a lot of hearts in September coming down the stretch."

On August 26 Mickey got three hits, a walk, and drove in three runs to beat the Senators. On August 29 Mel Stottlemyre, the newest Yankee pitching sensation, combined his efforts with Mantle to beat the Red Sox again. Now the Yanks were just three games behind the leading Orioles.

Mickey had heard of a new type of elastic-foam wrapping and suggested to the Yankee trainer that he wrap his bad legs in that type of bandage. His new bandages gave him much greater support and freedom and he was ready for the final pennant drive.

Above: Manager Berra and his ace pitcher, Whitey Ford, check the World Series Encyclopedia to find out Whitey's pitching record in the annual classic.

Opposite page: Mickey Mantle steps on the plate, followed by Roger Maris, who clouted a home run. Tiger coach Jimmy Dykes trudges to the mound to pull reliever Hank Aguirre during eighth inning of Detroit-New York game. Welcoming the runners is Yogi Berra. Yanks beat the Tigers, 7-3.

The race for the American League pennant was a seesaw battle. By mid-September, Mickey Mantle, Hector Lopez, John Blanchard, and Roger Maris hit the ball hard, and pitchers Jim Bouton with 18 wins, Whitey Ford with 17, and Al Downing with 13 continued to play inspired ball to lead the Yankees to victories.

On September 18 Mantle collected three base hits as the Yankees climbed back into first place, and on October 3 the Yankees clinched their fifth straight pennant.

This was a marvelous year for the Yankees. It was a triumphant year for their freshman manager, Yogi Berra, who led the injury-laden Yanks to another successful season. And it was another fine year for Mickey Mantle.

Mantle's battered legs had prevented him from playing for days at a time. Yet he appeared in 143 games; smashed out 141 hits; and had a batting average of .303, fourth leading in the American League.

Left to right: Whitey Ford won 17 games during the 1964 season, with a number of vital wins late in the season.

Bobby Richardson was a standout late in the 1964 season; the Yankees needed his bat for the run at another pennant.

By September 18, with Mickey Mantle clobbering opposing pitchers, Ralph Terry winning key games, and Tommy Tresh and Bob Richardson driving in runs in close games, the Yankees climbed back into first place in the American League race.

They began to call Jim Bouton "Bulldog" as the Yanks began their drive for the 1964 pennant. And Bouton responded, winning 18 games.

On gimpy legs much of the time, Mickey amazed his mates and Yankee fans as he bashed out 35 home runs and scored 92 times, and his fielding in the outfield was adequate.

And it was a fighting ballclub that manager Berra led into the World Series against an intrepid St. Louis Cardinal club and their outstanding manager, Johnny Keane.

It was a rugged Series for the Yankees as they battled an inspired Cardinal team that had such stars as Bob Gibson, Lou Brock, Tim McCarver, Curt Simmons, Curt Flood, Ken Boyer. They all performed brilliantly as they defeated the Yanks in a World Series that went the full seven games.

And it was a courageous Mickey Mantle, performing in one of his greatest World Series, on legs that seemingly would crumble at any moment, who was the "star of stars." Mickey slammed on one of the longest home runs ever seen at Yankee Stadium, a drive that traveled more that 475 feet in game three off pitcher Barney Schultz. In game six, at Busch Stadium in St. Louis, Roger Maris homered the Cards' hurler Curt Simmons, and Mantle followed with another towering home run— his 17th in World Series play.

In the seventh game, Richardson and Maris singled in a busy sixth inning, and heroic Mickey Mantle limped up to the plate, took one lethal swing, and the ball shot out of the field of play into the center-field stands for a glorious home run, giving the Yankees a temporary lead in this final game.

But that was all the runs that marvelous Bob Gibson allowed, and the Yanks went down fighting by a 7–5 margin. The Cardinals were World Champions.

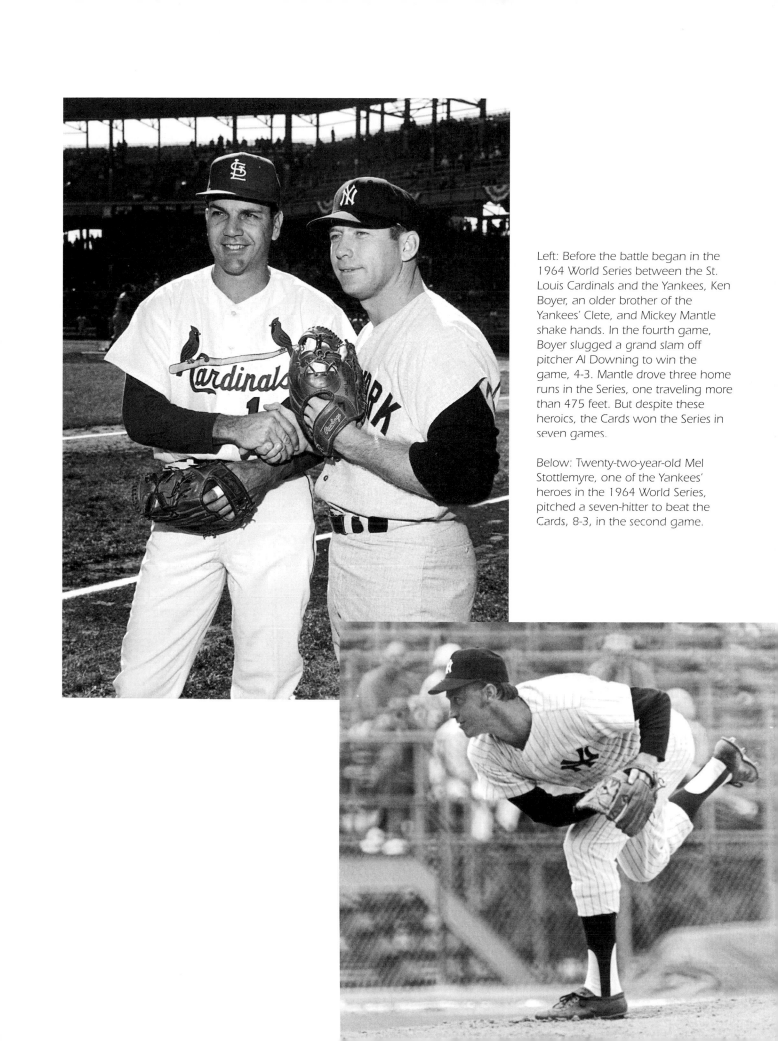

Left: Before the battle began in the 1964 World Series between the St. Louis Cardinals and the Yankees, Ken Boyer, an older brother of the Yankees' Clete, and Mickey Mantle shake hands. In the fourth game, Boyer slugged a grand slam off pitcher Al Downing to win the game, 4-3. Mantle drove three home runs in the Series, one traveling more than 475 feet. But despite these heroics, the Cards won the Series in seven games.

Below: Twenty-two-year-old Mel Stottlemyre, one of the Yankees' heroes in the 1964 World Series, pitched a seven-hitter to beat the Cards, 8-3, in the second game.

The two managers who startled the sports world after the World Series, Yogi Berra, left, ex-Yankees manager, and Johnny Keane, formally of the St. Louis Cardinals. They're pondering reporters' questions in this photo.

In one of the strangest switches ever made in the major leagues, St. Louis manager Johnny Keane resigned after his team had won the pennant and World Series in 1964, then was named manager of the Yankees for 1965.

Mantle's three towering home runs gave him a record of 18 home runs in World Series play.

But the curtain did not come down with that final out of the World Series. It was only a matter of days after the World Series that Johnny Keane resigned as Cardinal manager.

A day later, Yogi Berra was dismissed as the Yankee manager. His successor was Johnny Keane.

How had this all happened?

The general feeling in the clubhouse after the World Series was that the Yankees should have easily beaten the Cardinals. That was always the feeling when the Yankees lost.

"We'll get 'em next year," Yogi Berra said.

Under Yogi's direction the Yankees had come within one game of winning the Series during a year when such players as Joe Pepitone, Bobby Richardson, and Tony Kubek were subpar. Tommy Tresh was inconsistent, Maris did not play well until September, and Mantle was in and out of the lineup.

Early in the year, Ralph Houk was not happy with the Yankees' play under Berra, disliked his handling of the team and the lack of discipline under him, and set out to talk to the Cardinals' manager, Johnny Keane. Ralph finally broke down Keane's resistance and suggested that Keane quit the Cards and take over. The rest, as they say, is history.

There was no doubt about it: the Yankee players were unhappy about the treatment of Yogi Berra. Although a few players had made fun of Berra's choice of language and his mannerisms, he knew his baseball better than most big-league managers, and they were not happy with Johnny Keane.

Keane, a strict traditionalist and very religious, wanted to win every game in spring training. "Hell," said Jim Bouton, "most of us couldn't care less about winning those games. That was fun time. We'd be in bars every night, drinking and carousing, and then this new manager would hold a meeting and say, 'Look, there are about five players who are getting careless about this training.'

"Hell," said Bouton, "there were twenty-five guys getting careless and they began to complain to Ralph Houk about this new manager. It got so bad that we used to sit at another team meeting," said Bouton, "and practically laugh ourselves sick."

That's the way things looked as the season began in 1965.

"I began to feel that I was truly headed downhill," said Mantle, "and I took a lot of the blame myself. My shoulder, which I thought was pretty much healed, began to bother me again, and no amount of treatment seemed to help. It took me a long time to admit it, but I just couldn't uncork those long throws anymore. I used to love to bang those balls in

The Yankee infield in 1965: Clete Boyer, third base; Tony Kubek, short-stop; Bobby Richardson, second base; and Joe Pepitone, first base.

from deep center field, but in 1965 I only threw in when I really had to. I had to have help on every throw."

As the regular season began, Whitey Ford was fighting a battle against a constantly sore arm, Roger Maris was having trouble hitting the ball, and Mantle had those bad legs.

And Johnny Keane was going out of his mind trying to move his players around like in a checkers game. In center field he had Tommy Tresh instead of Mantle, who had trouble tracking those line drives, and had Mickey in left field. Maris would play right field or switch with Tresh.

As the season opened, the Yankees had Joe Pepitone on first base, Bobby Richardson at second, Tony Kubek at short, Clete Boyer on third, Johnny Blanchard was the catcher, and Mel Stottlemyre was on the mound.

Early in the season Maris broke a bone in his hand, and Keane and Maris had angry words after Johnny tried to play Roger with his bad hand. Clete Boyer punched out a guy in Fort Lauderdale and was in the manager's doghouse. Ellie Howard injured his back, and Joe Pepitone hated Keane so much he refused to play for him. All of a sudden the Yankees were falling apart.

When his shoulders and legs allowed him to, Mickey was in left field and played as well as he could. At the plate it was not until April 3 that he hit his third home run. But the Yankees lost to Minnesota, 7–3.

Mickey was out of the lineup early in May and sat out several games. It was the same old trouble, his legs and shoulder.

One May day, after a tough loss to the Twins, the players were sitting around, talking about their play.

"It's a different team without Mickey in there," said Boyer. "When he's out in center field, you can feel his presence. It's all the difference."

Ellie Howard came back with, "Mickey is the spirit of this team. He makes us want to win. He fights hard all the time and with all those injuries he ought to be in the hospital."

"You're right," said Joe Pepitone, "but there's something you guys are overlooking. Mickey is one of the kindest, most gracious guys in the world. I love the guy. I had been having trouble at home and got separated from my wife. I was living from one paycheck to another, broke all the time. I borrowed some money from Mickey, and when I went to pay him back, he said, 'Forget it.' Then he said to me one day, 'Look Joe, I've got a suite at the St. Moritz Hotel, you come on and live with me there. When you have your meals, just sign my name.' And I stayed with Mickey more than a month. . . .

"He took me everywhere with him and paid for everything," said Pepi. "He wouldn't let me take a penny out of my pocket. And he just got involved with me, told me everything. He'd come home after a game and he'd break down and cry. He'd cry about how he thought he would die at a young age. About how his father and grandfather died before forty years of age. He was actually sobbing," said Joe, "sitting there with his head in his hands. And I'd grab him and hug him. I'd say, 'Mick, come on now, man. Hey, you're going to live a long, long time.' And the last few years he played, I never saw him leave the hotel room. He'd never go out on the street. He couldn't walk a step what with a hundred people stopping him. I recall one day we went to the Tower East. I was dressed all in black with dark glasses and we sat down and whenever anyone came to our table, I would look at them and growl, 'Hey, get away. He don't want to be bothered. Understand?' And they left. They thought I was his bodyguard. I swear it."

By June 5 the Yankees, once the mightiest, were in ninth place, ten games off the pace of the leading Twins.

On June 8 the Yankee front office announced that there was going to be a "Mickey Mantle Day" at the Stadium to honor the 15 years that Mantle had been with the team.

"It's a great thing," said catcher Ellie Howard, "but at the same time I hope it doesn't mean that this is Mickey's way of saying good-bye."

Was this really a prelude to the departure of the great Mickey Mantle?

The date for Mickey Mantle Day was September 18, very close to the end of the season.

"HOW MUCH LONGER CAN HE GO ON?" was a headline in the *New York Post*.

On July 3 Johnny Keane talked to the press about spotting Mickey—that is, playing Mickey every other day.

However by the middle of July, Mickey was back in the lineup every day, hitting home runs occasionally and making his presence felt.

But one man isn't the complete ballclub. There were other players who played well for a few days, then flickered out. There was Mel Stottlemyre, who would go on to win 20 games in his first full season as a Yankee starter, and Whitey Ford, sore arm and all, winning 16 games and Al Downing and Bill Stafford and Jim Bouton.

As the great day dawned, Mickey Mantle Day, Mickey's personal idol, Joe DiMaggio, flew in from San Francisco for the occasion. And it was Joltin' Joe who introduced Mickey at the Stadium, jammed with more than 50,000 fans for the occasion.

Fifty thousand fans were on their feet, 50,000 fans shouting their throats raw, and all the disappointment with the showing of the 1965 New York Yankees was momentarily forgotten. The crowd had come to pay homage to a champion, and they paid it lustily as best they knew how to the man who had played 2,000 games for the New York club, given it everything he had, and thrilled the whole sports world with his performance.

Here was a man to honor. Here was a man of heart. Here was a man of courage. Here was a ballplayer for all time.

Mickey was at the microphone in the huge Stadium. The shouting of the fans would not let up. He waited. The shouting simmered down slowly, stopped for a moment, and Mickey spoke.

He thanked the fans.

"I want to thank Dan Topping and George Weiss," he said quietly, "for allowing me to play with the Yankees for fifteen years."

Again, the great shout of approval from the 50,000 fans.

"My one ambition," said Mickey after the pause, with the modesty that was his, "my one ambition is to play another fifteen years for the Yankees in New York."

To celebrate "Mickey Mantle Day" on June 8, 1965, Joe DiMaggio flew in from San Francisco. DiMaggio introduced Mantle to the huge crowd that had come to pay tribute to Mickey. Here in the photo, DiMaggio and Mickey wave to the fans as they walk around the Stadium.

The fans reacted as fans all over the baseball world react. They were up on their feet again, all 50,000 of them, and their great shouts echoed through the Stadium, throughout the whole baseball world.

But there were more words from Mickey. Perhaps one of the most moving moments in baseball history was still to come.

The shouting finally died down, and Mickey was at the microphone again. "If you fans won't mind," he said most quietly, "it would make me happy if all your gifts, all the gifts you have given me, all your donations, were turned over to the Hodgkin's Disease Foundation."

There was a great hush in the Stadium now. Throats clogged up and big men as well as little women, fought against the tears that came to their eyes.

Mickey's father, his wonderful father, had died of Hodgkin's disease at a comparatively young age. Mickey was paying tribute to that father and, at that moment, 50,000 fans in Yankee Stadium paid silent tribute with him.

"Thank you," said Mickey, and, for a moment, it was as if Mickey stood alone, surrounded by all his good friends, 50,000 of them. Then once more the thunder of the crowd rose in loud and honest approval, respect, gratitude, and love for the baseball hero throughout his 15 seasons as a Yankee.

No, the Yankees didn't have a good year in 1965, but the fans and Mickey had that one big day. It was a day no one would forget. The one negative note in that beautiful celebration: Would Mickey be back in a Yankee uniform in 1966?

"But at the time, as long as I was carrying my weight at the plate, I did not fret too much," said Mickey, "although I had to admit my injuries sure seemed to be piling up. My average stayed up pretty well, but the runs-scored production and my runs batted in tumbled down below what I had done in my first year as a Yankee. And my 19 home runs were the least I ever collected, except for my first year and the year in which I appeared in only 65 games.

"But 1965 was certainly my lowest point, and I began for the first time thinking of retiring from the game.

"That fall, however, I really did a job on myself. Back home in Dallas, I did a lot of hunting and fishing and played a lot of golf and my legs were beginning to feel good.

"One day I was playing football, with my brothers Ray and Butch against Mickey, Jr. and me. The game grew hot. I got caught up in the spirit so that when Butch dodged by me with the ball I made a wild lunge, bad shoulder or not, and put the tag on him. And man, that shoulder started to hurt like hell. I knew without being told that I had wrecked it. For a couple of weeks I kept the secret to myself, thinking I could work it out. Nothing doing," said Mickey.

"I phoned Ralph. Told him that I could not possibly play ball anymore. I couldn't lift the shoulder. We talked awhile, then Ralph told me to come to New York to see him and discuss the future.

"I got to New York, met Ralph, and he listened to me and looked at my bad shoulder. Then he suggested that as a personal favor, I should go to the Mayo Clinic in Rochester for a complete exam, and to please Houk I did just that.

"After the most complete physical exam, the doctors said that my trouble was a simple case of bone chips and calcium deposits and were curable by an operation.

"It was a long but not a serious or dangerous operation, and it left me with a scar from my shoulder to my biceps muscle, and before a couple of weeks had passed I found that I could move and throw the ball with little pain. A couple more weeks and I was able to swing a bat and I was ready for another season.

"At least I did not have to worry about my position on the team, for I had another year on my contract—a contract that began to pay me $100,000 a year plus certain expenses, and I hoped that players like Maris, Ellie Howard, Jim Bouton, Whitey Ford, Al Downing, and Mel Stottlemyre would be injury-free and we might have another shot at the pennant."

20

IN LAST PLACE

This was the year the Yankees fell totally apart, the summer the Yankees owned the cellar. It began with 16 losses in the first 20 games in 1966, and it finally ended in September with the former champions in tenth place, the first time the Yanks had ever viewed the American League from the bottom since 1912, when they were called the Highlanders.

"This was an extremely unhappy ballclub," said pitcher Jim Bouton. "Everybody was in a bad mood most of the time, and it seemed that everybody was rubbing each other the wrong way."

When the Yankees' 1966 record reached 4 and 6, general manager Ralph Houk fired Johnny Keane and stepped into the manager's post himself. Houk had won pennants in 1961, 1962, and 1963, and the team lineup still had Mickey Mantle, Roger Maris, and Tom Tresh patrolling the outfield. The infield of Joe Pepitone, Bobby Richardson, Clete Boyer and Ellie Howard, the catcher, was still in good shape, and the pitchers included Whitey Ford, Jim Bouton, Mel Stottlemyre, Al Downing, Hal Reniff, and Steve Hamilton. Only shortstop Tony Kubek was missing, and he was replaced by Horace Clarke.

But the chemistry had gone sour, and Maris, Ford, Boyer, and Bouton couldn't shake the team. Neither could the new manager, Ralph Houk, check the downhill slide.

Then Mickey Mantle returned to the lineup and began to pound the ball. In 12 days, Mickey hit 10 home runs and then had to leave the lineup with an assorted set of injuries.

MAN FOR ALL SEASONS . . . THAT'S MICKEY MANTLE was the headline story by John Carmichael of the *New York Post*.

But after that Mantle splurge of home runs, bringing his total to 488 homers in his career, the Yankees were in total disarray. They never got off the ground in 1966, but the fans turned out at the Stadium, and if you should ask them why, they would tell you that Babe Ruth built the Stadium with his home-run bat.

Lou Gehrig and Joe Dimaggio provided additional magic with their long drives and thrilling play, and Mickey Mantle . . . it was his big bat, his great speed, and his all-around brilliance throughout 16 years that packed the Stadium. And it was still Mantle attempting to stem the tide at this late date.

"I've seen him bandaged from thigh to knee on both his legs," wrote John Carmichael. "He had a bone chip taken from a shoulder six months ago, and he was still out in center field on Opening Day last April. He couldn't throw. Infielders had to race to the outfield to take his relays. But in July he hit ten homers, and eight more in the first six games in August!

"In the 1961 World Series in Cincinnati, Mantle had to go back to the bench after banging out a single because there was blood seeping out of his uniform, blood from a wound. They'll have to tear the uniform off him before that Mickey finally turns in his glove!"

When the Yankees dropped 16 of their first 20 games in 1966, Johnny Keane was fired and Ralph Houk took over as the manager. Houk had won pennants in 1961, 1962 and 1963. But the chemistry was missing, and Houk could not move the team. Despite heroic efforts by a gimpy Mickey Mantle and Roger Maris, the Yankees were in disarray.

No wonder the fans cheered for him! No wonder the fans gave Mickey Mantle an ovation every time they could. Truly, he was a man for all seasons.

Like a number of other top 500 corporations the Columbia Broadcasting System was into an expansion era, going conglomerate with such subsidiaries as publishing houses and toy companies. So why not a ballclub? The network had close to $100 million sitting around waiting for an attractive investment. So they brought the Yankees for $14.4 million and sold it ten years later for $10 million.

As president of the Yankees, Mike Burke had been given clearance to "rid the Yankees," clean out the players not producing, trade them, and start winning some games.

A championship season for the Yankees in 1964 had been followed by a disaster into tenth place, so Burke traded Roger Maris, the great home run hero of yesteryear, to the Cardinals for a journeyman player few had ever heard of. Roger had been hurt several times in 1965, had hit just eight home runs, and in 1966 Roger followed with 13 homers, so they let him go to St. Louis—where he promptly helped the Cards to pennants in 1967 and 1968.

In October Burke released Hector Lopez, the Yankees' foremost utility player, who had played in five World Series. A month later Clete Boyer, an eight-year Yankee, was shipped to Atlanta. Bobby Richardson retired, and Tony Kubek quit.

Thus the 1967 lineups were patchwork quilts of hacks, youngsters, one superstar in Mickey Mantle—and were doomed to another dismal season.

There was one exciting note as the Yankees assembled in Fort Lauderdale for their spring training. Manager Ralph Houk had plans for Mickey Mantle that surprised everyone.

There was a new first baseman for the Yankees in their 1967 spring training session in Fort Lauderdale. It was an old Yankee but a new place for him. It was none other than that former great slugging outfielder, Mickey Mantle.

It was Ralph Houk's idea. It was a great idea. It had everybody wondering why nobody had thought of it before.

A first baseman has less ground to cover, is less mobile, has less throwing to do—or, at least, shorter distances to throw. It was obvious that Mickey's injured legs could no longer cover the outfield the way they once did, and that his arm couldn't get the ball back to the infield the way it used to do.

Mickey Mantle fields a ground ball as the New York Yankees start their spring training at Fort Lauderdale. The Yankees are giving Mantle a try at first base instead of his regular outfield post to ease the strain on his ailing legs.

"First base! That's the solution to the problem!"

Of course, it wasn't that easy. A big-league first baseman has to have a lot of know-how around the bag. He has to know how to play batters close to the line, pivot and throw to second for the double play, take hard-hit grounders, judge infield pop-ups—a thousand and one different things that are different from playing the outfield. He would be in virtually every play.

How would Mickey do in this strange position?

"It's very simple," said Houk optimistically. "All he has to do is find the bag, cover it, and catch the ball."

"How about all those little stop-and-go movements?" asked reporters. "Won't they prove more of a strain on his legs? And what about covering and moving on the double play?"

"Don't tell me that you're worried about Mickey," said the Yankee skipper.

There was no answer to that. All the sportswriters could do was to sit back and watch.

Joe Pepitone was around the sack, giving Mickey pointers. "Pretty, pretty!" yelled Whitey Ford, encouraging the freshman first baseman. "You look better than Dick Stuart already, Mick!"

Stuart was a first baseman who was called everything from Stone Hands to Dr. Strangeglove because of all the errors he made playing the bag. Whitey, of course, was kidding. It was part of the game. It all was meant to encourage the great slugger, and it did. Mickey did all right at first base, and it gave his bat new life at the plate.

With the beginning of the pennant race, the fans had a new dramatic moment in store for them. Mickey was going to aim for that 500-home-run circle, a circle of players which contained only five names. Babe Ruth headed the list with the probably unbeatable 714 career home runs. The amazing Willie Mays of the San Francisco Giants was second, with 546 homers to his credit. The legendary Jimmie Foxx, who was to die in July of that year, was third with 534. Ted Williams of Boston Red Sox fame was next with 521. Mel Ott, that great Giant of old, was fifth with 511 home runs to his credit. Could Mickey Mantle become the sixth? Would his legs and arms hold out long enough for him to reach and enter that brilliant circle of great major-league sluggers?

The 1967 Yankees weren't much better than the 1966 Yankees. There were spurts now and then when Mantle was playing, and the fans began to cheer their heroes on. But then the losing streaks became all too common, and all hope would be dashed.

Mickey Mantle, switching to first base tried on a new glove after signing his third $100,000 contract.

The 1967 Yankees' lineup included Horace Clarke at second base; Ruben Amaro at short; and Ellie Howard as the catcher until August, when he was traded to Boston; Steve Whitaker in right field, Joe Pepitone in center field; and Tom Tresh in left field. The new first baseman was Mickey Mantle.

Mickey Mantle quickly adjusted to his new position, and as the season progressed he began to hit the ball with some of his old skills. He slugged his 497th homer in the fifth game of the season, then his 498th and his 499th, and the fans began to clamor for the fabled 500th homer.

Now it was May 14 and Mickey, still with his heart set on the 500th blast, took the field against the Orioles.

The game turned into a seesaw thriller. Now it was 6–6 with Stu Miller, a slick curveball pitcher, on the mound for the Orioles.

Mickey had never hit a home run off Miller and now was up to hit; the count was 3–2, and a big crowd was up and shouting for Mickey to hit.

Miller made all kinds of tricky moves on the mound. He bobbed his head, pumped his shoulder, wiggled his hips, and hurled the pitch to the plate. It was a bit high and Mickey didn't waste any time. He stepped into the ball and smashed it into the left-field bleachers for a home run.

In the Yankee dugout, Tommy Tresh, soaking his injured ankle in an ice bucket, jumped to his feet, cracked his head on the cement ceiling of the dugout, but yelled his head off. Every other Yankee in the dugout was cheering as well.

Above: Mickey Mantle poses with Louis de Fillippo of Mount Vernon, New York, after a game at Yankee Stadium. The ball held by the youth was the ball Mantle belted into the lower right field stands for his 500th career homer. Mantle hit the ball off Stu Miller of the Baltimore Orioles in the seventh inning.

Opposite page: Mickey Mantle connects for his 536th home run, sending the ball into the right-field stands in the third inning of a game with the Boston Red Sox September 20, 1968, at Yankee Stadium. That made 18 homers for Mantle that season. Boston won, 4-3.

"It's out of here!" yelled Tresh. "It's a homer! Number 500!"

The 40,000 fans cheered Mickey every step of the way as he gingerly touched each base. As he reached the Yankee dugout, Ralph Houk was the first to grab and hug him, and each Yankee player took his turn shaking the slugger's hand. The roar of the crowd continued in a cascade of sound that seemed like a thunderclap.

"A thing like that stirs you up inside," said Houk. "A kind of chill creeps up and down your spine."

A thrill to remember.

Mickey Mantle had hit his 500th home run.

"In May 1968 I hit home run number 522, putting me ahead of my idol, Ted Williams," said Mantle.

"My last home run came on September 20. Number 536. It was two more than Jimmie Foxx. Then a week later I came up to hit against Boston at Fenway Park, made an out, and sat down. In the dugout, Ralph

Houk sent in a new kid, Andy Kosco, to replace me. I finally realized it was the end of the line.

"After a few minutes, I headed for the locker room, took off my uniform, and went home," said Mantle.

"The following year, in 1969, I tried my darndest to play another year," said Mickey. "I went down to Fort Lauderdale much earlier than any of the other regulars and tried to work out—just a little running and throwing. But I just couldn't do it. I was absolutely convinced that I no longer could play at the level I wanted.

"There was no use in putting off my retirement.

"The night before the Yankees announced a press conference, I went out to dinner with Merlyn and Harold and Stella Youngman, my great pals and business partner in Commerce. Baseball was all I had ever known," said Mickey, "and I was in no mood for any celebration."

The next day, March 1, before a battery of more than a hundred newspapermen and sportscasters, Mickey Mantle simply faced the crowd and said, "This is it. I can't run like I used to, can't throw, and I guess that after eighteen years, I've had it. Thanks, fellas, for your support."

With that, Mickey drove out to the ballpark, packed his duffel bag, said a few good-byes, then left the Yankees.

21

THE HALL OF FAME
PHONE CALL

Finally, after a couple of weeks back home in Dallas, I realized that my $100,000 salary was gone, my bowling alley had closed up. Here I was now, thirty-seven years old with a big family to take care of. What was I going to do?

"When you're a big-league star for eighteen years, you never have to do anything for yourself," said Mickey.

From the moment a big leaguer awakens in the morning to bedtime, he is served like a king. His slightest wish is carried out. He always has a younger player order his food, go on errands, find a cab to the ballpark. At the park, the Yankee trainer takes care of his uniform, sees to it that he is properly bandaged, bathes and massages his injured legs and shoulders. Everything is taken care of.

Now, at home, he is suddenly an ordinary person, and he is hurt when his wife says, "Mickey, would you please take the garbage out?"

Fortunately for Mickey, he had the good sense to defer half his $100,000 salary during the past five years, so he had more than $250,000 safely in the bank.

In the summer of 1968 Mickey and half a dozen investors began to develop a new restaurant venture one, that would feature country home chicken, chicken fried steaks, biscuits, and other southern foods. The first restaurant opened in San Antonio and was doing so well that the investors filed with the SEC and the company went public. Soon there were some thirteen Mickey Mantle Country Cookin' restaurants, and all were doing a solid business.

"As chairman of the board," said Mickey, "I had 110,000 shares of stock, and when the company went public at $15 per share, I thought I was set for life."

But shortly after the company went public, business went sour, and one by one the restaurants closed down.

By February 1970, Mickey went down to spring training to see his old buddies, and Ralph Houk asked him if he would like to be a Yankee coach. He had missed the sounds and sights so much.

Mickey took the job offer, but when he finally put on a Yankee uniform and took his coaching position at first base, he realized it was purely a public relations ploy. He had no business as a coach; the players joked about it, and after a few weeks Mickey left to go back home.

Now he realized that he was still thinking of a comeback.

"Back home," said Mickey, "I'd be okay for a week or so, then I'd turn into a caged lion and I would dream of playing ball again." Mickey's fantasy went something like this:

> The sun came out early and hot. Tom Johnson, head groundkeeper of the Yankees, sat in his underground office and looked over his schedule for the day. The phone rang.
>
> "Johnson here."
>
> "You'd better get out to the field," an assistant said.
>
> "There's a guy wandering around out there. It looks fishy, so I thought I'd let you know."
>
> "Thanks," Johnson said, quickly putting down the receiver. There had been some peculiar things happening around Yankee Stadium lately, and he wanted to see what was going on.
>
> He got up and hurried out onto the field. Shading his eyes against the strong sun, he could see a figure in a business suit near the center-field wall. Trotting briskly across the field, Johnson yelled:
>
> "Hey, you! What're you doing here? Better get off the field, there's a game tonight. I got to get the crew working on the field."
>
> The man turned and Johnson could see that it was Mantle.
>
> "Why, Mickey, what are you doing here so early? You and the rest of the players don't get here until about ten-thirty. It's only nine now."
>
> "Hi, Tom. I was just looking over these plaques on the wall here, readin' what it says on them."
>
> Mickey didn't have to point to the plaques. Johnson, the Yankee team, and the Yankee fans knew all about them. Knew them by heart. There were four of them at the time, honoring the greatest players of all time—all the Yankee stars.
>
> One plaque honored Babe Ruth, the greatest player of them all.

Another told the feats of the "Iron Horse," the great Lou Gehrig. The third was for Miller Huggins, the crafty manager of the Yankee team in the Ruth era. The fourth was for Joe DiMaggio, the "Yankee Clipper," the marvelous centerfielder in the late thirties, forties, and early fifties.

"You know, Tom," Mickey said in his fantasy, "there are times when I wake up in the middle of the night and I pinch myself. I say to myself, 'Mickey, did this all really happen to you? Just a kid from Commerce, who worked in the mines? Was I really a Yankee? Did I really get to play with the great DiMaggio?' Then I get down here early, to prove to myself that it's all really true. You know, I read now and then about this writer and that one says I'm up here with these greats." Mickey nodded. "Not me, Tom. I'm just thrilled to death every time I put on that Yankee uniform and get out there to play. I'm the luckiest guy alive."

"It ain't hard to see how you feel, Mick, but it's true."

Tom Johnson had seen and talked with a lot of players. Some he liked, and some not so much. There were all kinds of players, just as among people in general. But he'd always had a special feeling for Mantle. And this morning he felt fonder and closer to the youngster than ever before.

"I've been standing here, thinking of all the people who helped me make my way," Mickey said. "My dad, Mutt. I can't tell you how much I miss him. I think about him every time I play. And Gramps, the best grandpa a fella ever had. And Casey—well, everybody knows he has been like another father to me. And then there was Barney Barnett and Tom Greenwade . . . so many others. Heck, without them I'd still be workin' in the mines."

Johnson just listened. He knew exactly what Mickey was trying to say. Johnson knew about the amazing story of the rise of the poor miner's son to the top place on the top team.

"And now," said Mickey, "when I think that Casey's got me battin' in the cleanup position—that's Joe DiMaggio's spot—well, you can't blame me for wonderin' if I'm dreamin`."

Then Mantle started for the clubhouse, and Johnson walked along. In the dressing room, Mickey peeled off his coat.

"I might as well try on my new uniform," he said. "I hope it's good and roomy."

Then after he had it on he said, "Tom, how's it look?"

Johnson stared at Mickey with an expert's eye. Then he smiled. "On you the Yankee uniform looks great. It *fits*."

The weeks quickly passed for Mickey Mantle as he raced from one end of the country to the other to attend the numerous dinners, banquets and golf celebrity tournaments for which he was paid very well. But he was bored. There was nothing like the excitement on the diamond at Yankee Stadium, and he often dreamed of those days . . . gone but not forgotten.

Then the Claridge Hotel in Atlantic City offered him a post as the "official greeter for the hotel." Mickey was to host parties for big gamblers from out of the country who attended golf tournaments, as the Claridge representative. The job paid very well, $100,000 plus expenses, and it put an end to his worries about some financial security for his large family.

Then all of a sudden there was an explosion that took place in the sports world. Suddenly there was a tremendous demand for baseball memorabilia of all kinds—cards, photographs, signed autographs. At an auction, a Mickey Mantle baseball card that sold for a few dollars in 1952 was sold for $8,500. A Honus Wagner baseball card was sold for $450,000 at an auction at Sotheby's. The memorabilia business was now caught up in a tidal wave of expansion, and soon there were conventions and huge shows all over the country selling all kinds of baseball memorabilia.

To boost attendance at these shows, top baseball stars were paid thousands of dollars for a few hours to sign autographs, and most of the big stars, such as Joe DiMaggio, Willie Mays, and Yogi Berra, eagerly attended these shows and were paid very well.

When Mickey Mantle let it be known that he would be interested in appearing at such memorabilia shows, every company in the business besieged him with calls for his appearance. He was so overwhelmed with offers that Mickey turned his affairs over to a management agency, and soon for a fee of from $15,000 to $20,000 per appearance he was busy twelve months a year.

Ofttimes such appearances included a celebrity golf tournament, where Mickey would play a round of golf with a local personage for an additional fee. He would shake hands, have his picture taken, have a few drinks, have dinner, more drinks. . . . Usually the drinking would go on and on until the wee hours. Year after year this continued.

The drinking bouts were not something new for Mickey, for when he was an active player, he and Billy Martin and Whitey Ford were on the cabaret scene almost nightly. And there were times when Mickey was so hung over, he would not start a ball game, and would sit on the bench far away from Stengel's glaring eye. Casey did not bother Mickey too much about his postgame carousing, for he had been a notorious boozer in his own right when he was an active player.

On July 15, 1974, there was a memorable phone call from the Associated Press to Mickey Mantle at his Dallas home. When Mickey hung up the receiver he let out the loudest war whoop ever heard in the Mantle household.

"That was the AP!" Mickey yelled to Merlyn and other Mantle family members. "Me and Whitey Ford are voted into the Baseball Hall of Fame!"

"I can't believe it's true!" he yelled again and again. "Me and Whitey.

Above: Mickey Mantle, together with Whitey Ford, after being elected to the Baseball Hall of Fame.

Left: Mickey Mantle and Whitey Ford, longtime Yankee teammates, on January 16, 1974, new Hall of Fame members. Mantle became only the seventh player in history to be elected to the Hall of Fame in his first year of eligibility, drawing a total of 322 votes of the 365 ballots cast by members of the Baseball Writers' Association of America.

Below: At the Hall of Fame induction ceremonies, Mickey Mantle, Whitey Ford, Cool Papa Bell and umpire Jocko Conlon.

In the Hall of Fame, and together. How about that? This is an impossible dream, and it came true."

"That phone call was one of the greatest thrills of my entire life. It was something that I had secretly dreamed about," said Mickey, "but never thought it would happen."

The induction ceremony at Cooperstown, New York, was held on August 10, 1974. Mickey had chartered a bus from New York City, and Whitey chartered another for his family and pals. Mickey's group included his wife, Merlyn; his mother; the four Mantle boys; Mickey's lawyer, Roy True; Harold and Stella Youngman (Harold was Mickey's business partner in Commerce); the Phil Rizzutos; and several friends from Dallas and Commerce.

At the ceremony, held on the back porch of the Hall of Fame Museum and surrounded by the hills and mountains of Cherry Valley, and Lake Otsego, more than 10,000 persons traveled to the induction of Mickey and Whitey.

At the microphone, Mickey introduced his wife, mother, and sons, and thanked all of his Yankee teammates and especially Casey Stengel, who was present.

Opposite page: The years passed; there were hundreds of celebrity dinners, golf tours, and banquets, and they began to take their toll.

Above: Five of the greatest Yankees. At an Old-Timers' Day in 1985 (L-R) Billy Martin, Joe DiMaggio, Mickey Mantle, Whitey Ford, and Phil Rizzuto salute the flag.

"Later on," said Mickey, "when I traveled around the country, people would ask me about my greatest thrill. I had two such great thrills. When I put on my Yankee uniform for the first time in 1951, and then being voted into the Hall of Fame with Whitey. That has to be the greatest."

22

INTO THE HOSPITAL

One night Merlyn and Mickey were having dinner with Yogi Berra and his wife, Carmen. Both Berra and Mantle were drinking straight vodka on the rocks and were at it fast and furious. When dinner was over, Mickey got into the car at the driver's seat. Merlyn tried to push him over, and Yogi shouted, "Merlyn, I wouldn't let him drive. He's loaded."

But Mickey just sat there, started the car and roared off, pushing his new Lincoln to sixty-five miles per hour. Merlyn began to grab the wheel, but Mickey continued to push her away.

The pair continued to grapple; just then Mickey looked up as the car crashed head-on into a pole. The impact was tremendous. Merlyn was hurled through the windshield.

"Fortunately," said Mickey, "a local police officer, a neighbor and friend, was at the scene, and rushed Merlyn and me to the hospital." Merlyn had several stitches in her head, but was not too badly hurt. Mickey was badly shaken up, but in two or three days later was able to play ball.

The story never made the papers as our friend, the local cop, kept the story within the precinct.

"But," said Mickey, "the accident scared hell out of me, and I decided to do something about my drinking."

Several days later, Mickey discussed his problem with Pat Summerall, a Dallas friend and former football star with the Giants. Pat pushed Mickey to check himself into the Betty Ford Alcohol Abuse Center in 1994. Mickey finally did check into the clinic, was treated for a thirty-day period, and was released. Finally his drinking days were over—for good.

After his release from the Betty Ford Center he publicly acknowledged his alcoholism. But by then his doctors said his cirrhosis of the liver was "so advanced" that he was likely to need a transplant soon. "I'm not going to lie to you," a doctor told him then. "The next drink you take might very well be your last."

On May 28, 1995, Mickey checked into the Baylor University Medical Center in Texas with severe stomach pains that had persisted over several days.

Tests during a two-week period yielded a report that a cancerous tumor was blocking Mickey's bile ducts in his liver.

When the news of Mickey's illness hit the media, shock waves reverberated across the nation. Front-page stories told the news of Mickey's plight, and friends and sports fans all across the nation were plunged into despair. How could this happen to this great, big All-American hero? It seemed that in his career, Mantle had been injured and reinjured nearly every season. But somehow the Mickey Mantle of old would come back stronger and better than ever, leading the Yankees to one championship after another, for eighteen long years.

"He'll come through this," said sports fans across the country. "He'll beat this, too."

Mantle's illness threatened to become the final blow against a slugger whose epic home runs and boyish, blond looks had transfixed New York City and the nation. He had lost his best friend, Billy Martin, in an alcohol-related vehicular accident in 1989. In 1993, one of Mickey's four sons, Danny, sought treatment at the Betty Ford Center. Then another son, Billy, who had been suffering from Hodgkin's disease, collapsed and died of a heart attack at a drug and alcohol treatment center.

Mickey long feared that Hodgkin's disease, which killed his grandfather at age 40 and his father at age 39, would claim him at an early age. But as he grew older, he repeated what became his story line: "If I knew I was going to live this long," he said, "I'd have taken better care of myself."

On June 7, Mantle was admitted to the Baylor University Medical Center for treatment of his condition.

On June 8, doctors at the hospital told Mickey that he had to have a liver transplant within the next two to four weeks "if he wanted to live."

Mantle, too feeble to rise from his bed, fell silent at the grim news, but then lifted his head, smiled, and said to Dr. Robert Goldstein, "I want you to do whatever we have to do. It goes back to my days as a ballplayer. I NEVER GIVE UP."

On June 9, Mickey's doctors at the Baylor University Medical

Mickey Mantle gestures during a press conference at Baylor University Medical Center in Dallas, where he was admitted on June 7, 1995, for diagnosis and treatment of a stomach ailment. Several days later doctors told Mickey he had to have a liver transplant within the next four weeks.

Center removed Mickey's liver and made the transplant. But after removing Mickey's liver, they discovered that the cancer had already spread to his bile ducts, and from there probably elsewhere. But by then, they said, the vessels to his new liver had already been attached, so they had no choice but to proceed.

Within two days after the transplant, under a pathologist's microscope, the cancer cells proved to be the most dangerous his doctors had ever seen and were now attacking other parts of his body, including his heart and his new liver.

At this point Mickey was told that further treatments, including radiation and chemotherapy, were available but futile.

Mickey gamely asked only that his doctors relieve his terrible pain. His gastroenterologist, Dr. Dan DeMarco, knew that Mickey had but two to ten days left and offered to share his outlook with Mickey.

Mantle replied, "Don't even tell me how long I have to live."

As Mickey weakened from day to day, his three sons asked his former teammates to visit him and to say good-bye.

Whitey Ford flew in the same night, and Mickey was so cheered by Whitey's visit and his stories that he sat up in bed and traded jokes as if they were on a road trip. Whitey handed Mickey a baseball autographed by the 1995 Yankees. Tears came to Mickey's eyes as he held the ball.

Then in rapid succession as Moose Skowron, Hank Bauer, and Johnny Blanchard visited Mickey, he felt marvelous and looked well.

Merlyn Mantle was astounded to see her husband looking so well. "I thought you said he was very sick," she told Dr. DeMarco.

"I really thought he would pass away at any moment," said DeMarco, "but Whitey Ford made a liar out of me."

Bobby Richardson, a former teammate and now a lay minister, helped Mickey to pray and to accept his death with grace.

Then, shortly after 12:30 A.M. on August 13, Merlyn Mantle, at Mickey's bedside, called Dr. DeMarco to come immediately and told the doctor that Mickey had stopped breathing.

DeMarco arrived within minutes and pronounced Mickey dead. "I'm sorry," he said, turning to Merlyn and son David. "But he's out of pain. He's resting now."

The next day, the Yankees, engaged in a tight race for a postseason playoff spot, wore a black ribbon and Mickey's number, 7, on their left sleeve. There was a moment of silence before the game, and a moment of silence in all the ballparks across the nation. At Yankee Stadium there was a huge video remembrance of Mickey Mantle.

"Mickey Mantle, a Yankee forever," proclaimed the Stadium marquee. The scoreboard message simply read:

"NO. 7 WITH US FOREVER."

Opposite page: After the liver transplant, Mickey, barely able to lift his head, told his doctor, Dr. Robert Goldstein, "I want you fellows to do whatever we have to do. It goes back to my days as a player. I never give up."

THE STATISTICS

MILESTONES AND HIGHLIGHTS

Yankee debut: April 17, 1951

Triple Crown: 1956

A.L.M.V.P.: 1956, 1957, 1962

A.L. home run leader: 1955–56, 1958, 1960

Home runs: 536 (Eighth place)

Home runs from both sides of plate in same game: 10 times, A.L. record.

Grand slams: 9

Most games played for the Yankees: 2,401

Most at-bats for the Yankees: 8,102

Three home runs in one game: May 13, 1955

All-Star Game: 1952–65

Golden Glove: 1962

Uniform retired: June 8, 1969 (No. 7)

Elected to Baseball Hall of Fame: 1974

MICKEY MANTLE'S CAREER STATS

Regular Season

Year	G	AB	H	2B	3B	HR	R	RBI	BB	SO	BA	SA
1951	96	341	91	11	5	13	61	65	43	74	.267	.433
1952	142	549	171	37	7	23	94	87	75	111	.311	.530
1953	127	461	136	24	3	21	105	92	79	90	.295	.497
1954	146	543	163	17	12	27	129	102	102	107	.300	.525
1955	147	517	158	25	11	37	121	99	113	97	.306	.611
1956	150	533	188	22	5	52	132	130	112	99	.353	.705
1957	144	474	173	28	6	34	121	94	146	75	.365	.665
1958	150	519	158	21	1	42	127	97	129	120	.304	.592
1959	144	541	154	23	4	31	104	75	94	126	.285	.514
1960	153	527	145	17	6	40	119	94	111	125	.275	.558
1961	153	514	163	16	6	54	132	128	126	112	.317	.687
1962	123	377	121	15	1	30	96	89	122	78	.321	.605
1963	65	172	54	8	0	15	40	35	40	32	.314	.622
1964	143	465	141	25	2	35	92	111	99	102	.303	.591
1965	122	361	92	12	1	19	44	46	73	76	.255	.452
1966	108	333	96	12	1	23	40	56	57	76	.288	.538
1967	144	440	108	17	0	22	63	55	107	113	.245	.434
1968	144	435	103	14	1	18	57	54	106	97	.237	.398
Totals	2,401	8,102	2,415	344	72	536	1,677	1,509	1,734	1,710	.298	.557

World Series

Year	G	AB	H	2B	3B	HR	R	RBI	BB	SO	BA	SA
1951	2	5	1	0	0	0	1	0	2	1	.200	.200
1952	7	29	10	1	1	2	5	3	3	4	.345	.655
1953	6	24	5	0	0	2	3	7	3	8	.208	.458
1955	3	10	2	0	0	1	1	1	0	2	.200	.500
1956	7	24	6	1	0	3	6	4	6	5	.250	.667
1957	6	19	5	0	0	1	3	2	3	1	.263	.421
1958	7	24	6	0	1	2	4	3	7	4	.250	.583
1960	7	25	10	1	0	3	8	11	8	9	.400	.800
1961	2	6	1	0	0	0	0	0	0	2	.167	.167
1962	7	25	3	1	0	0	2	0	4	5	.120	.160
1963	4	15	2	0	0	1	1	1	1	5	.133	.333
1964	7	24	8	2	0	3	8	8	6	8	.333	.792
Totals	65	230	59	6	2	18	42	40	43	54	.257	.535

Reminiscences
and Farewells

My family lost a great friend and a truly wonderful person. Now that both Mickey and Billy are gone, I'll never have friends like them again in my life.

    —**Whitey Ford,** on former teammates Mantle and Billy Martin

He transcends any game and any team. Just as Jesse Owens was to track and field and Michael Jordan is to basketball, Mickey Mantle is to baseball.

    —**George Steinbrenner,** Yankee owner

I'll never forget how hard he played all the time, especially the catch he made in my perfect game.

    —**Don Larsen,** who pitched a perfect game in the 1956 World Series

He could run, throw, and hit. There's no telling how good he'd have been with two good legs.

    —**Yogi Berra,** former teammate

He was magnificent. His power, once in batting practice in spring training, I saw him hit the first nine pitches he got over the fence, It was effortless.

    —**Phil Linz,** whose locker was next to Mantle's

I'd rather he go than suffer. He suffered enough in his career.

—**Bill Skowron,** former Yankee first baseman

We lost a legend today, and I lost a real friend.

—**Mel Stottlemyre,** former Yankee pitcher

A Tale of Tape
and Tape Measures

Despite a career full of injuries, Mickey Mantle had a rare ability to power a baseball a long way. Even rarer, he could do it from both sides of the plate. He finished his career with 536 home runs: 373 as a left-handed batter and 163 batting right-handed. He also homered 18 times in the World Series, and no one hit more. Here are some of the more significant home runs Mantle muscled during his career as well as some of the more serious injuries that kept him taped up so often.

The Power and the Glory

May 1, 1951: Mantle, nineteen years old and batting left-handed, gets his first major-league home run, off Randy Gumpert of the Chicago White Sox

May 16, 1951: Batting right-handed against Dick Rozek of the Cleveland Indians, Mantle hits the first of his 266 homers at Yankee Stadium. No player has hit more there.

April 17, 1953: The tape measure becomes a figurative fixture after Mantle, batting right-handed, clubs a pitch from Chuck Stobbs of the Washington Senators out of Griffith Stadium. Best estimate: 565 feet.

Oct. 4, 1953: In Brooklyn, a bases-filled homer off the right-hander Russ Meyer in the fifth game makes Mantle only the fourth player, to that time, to hit a grand slam in the World Series.

May 13, 1955: Two homers from the left side off Steve Gromek and one from the right side off Bob Miller give Mantle a three-homer game against the Detroit Tigers at Yankee Stadium.

May 30, 1956: Another Washington Senator pitcher is tattooed as Mantle's high drive off right-hander Pedro Ramos hits the upper-deck facade in right field, a foot and a half short of going out of Yankee Stadium for a homer, something no major leaguer has ever done.

Oct. 8, 1956: Don Larsen grabs the spotlight with a 2–0 perfect game against the Brooklyn Dodgers in the fifth game of the World Series, but Mantle's homer off right-hander Sal Maglie and a running backhanded catch in deep left-center at the Stadium accent the feat.

May 22, 1963: Like Ramos seven years earlier, right-hander Bill Fischer of the Kansas City Athletics watches a pitch nearly leave the Stadium in right field. This one misses by three feet, but the ball is still rising when it hits the facade.

Oct. 10, 1964: With the score tied, 1–1, in Game 3 at the Stadium, Mantle leads off the Yankee ninth and laces the first pitch from knuckle-baller Barney Schultz of the St. Louis Cardinals into the upper deck in right field. It is his 16th World Series homer, surpassing Babe Ruth's mark that stood for 32 years.

Aug. 9, 1965: On the second pitch ever thrown in an indoor stadium, Mantle, batting leadoff, homers off Dick Farrell of Houston in an exhibition game that officially opens the Astrodome.

Sept. 20, 1968: Jim Lonborg of the Boston Red Sox is touched for a home run in the third inning at the Stadium. It is number 536, the last of Mantle's career.

The Big Hurt

High School: After being kicked in the left shin during football practice, Mantle develops osteomyelitis, an infection of the bone marrow that endangers his knee for years.

World Series, 1951: Catches his spikes on an outfield sprinkler cover in the second game and needs five months for the knee's torn ligaments to mend.

World Series, 1957: Milwaukee's Red Schoendienst falls on Mantle's right shoulder in a play at second. The injury hampers his throwing and lefty hitting.

September 1961: Falls out of the home-run race with Roger Maris with a virus and a hip abscess.

June 1963: Runs into an outfield fence, breaking his left foot and doing ligament damage to his left knee. Out of everyday lineup for three months.

INDEX